W9-ADA-500
College of St. Francis
JOLIET, ILL.

THE POEMS OF PROPERTIUS

Translated by

JOHN WARDEN

Scarborough College
University of Toronto

Copyright © 1972
The Bobbs-Merrill Company, Inc.
Printed in the United States of America
Library of Congress Catalog Card Number 77–169063
First Printing
Designed by Starr Atkinson

874.4
P965w

TO SUSAN

5-11-73

65766

CONTENTS

Foreword **ix**
Note on the Poet's Life **xi**
Select Bibliography **xii**
Note on the Text **xiv**

THE POEMS OF PROPERTIUS

Book One **3**
Book Two **47**
Book Three **133**
Book Four **187**
Glossary of Names **231**

FOREWORD

This is not an introduction. The poet should introduce himself in his own words. Translation makes this impossible; but if none of his qualities survive the transfer, no words of mine can now revive them.

For his words are very much his own, shifting, restless, always at work, exploiting ambiguity, straining at syntax, heightening meaning by collocation, blurring it by dislocation. His sensitive ear provides the music for this "dance of the intellect," and his vivid visual imagination illuminates the whole with shafts of light, sometimes disturbingly bright.

And the tone is a curious blend of irony and intensity. The central theme of his poetry, his love affair with Cynthia, is presented throughout from this double perspective: there is irony in the passion, there is passion in the irony. In another recurrent theme, his attempt to define his literary role and his attitude to the Augustan reconstruction, there is the same ambivalence, a flirting with Augustanism that stops short of commitment. Poem 4.1, with its strangely balanced but discordant members, is the most striking demonstration of this. Only in poem 4.6 does commitment appear to be total, and the absence of the undertow of irony makes this poem, for me at least, one of the less successful.

Poem 4.7 is perhaps the best example of these qualities in a fully developed form. Here the intensity of remembered love is ironically set against the poet's representation of himself, the conventional scenery gives objectivity to personal experience, the poet's imagination gives life and colour to the conventional scenery, pathos and domestic comedy stand cheek by jowl, myth and mis-en-scene are one and the same, and the whole is suffused with the macabre eroticism of death.

NOTE ON THE POET'S LIFE

Sextus Propertius was born sometime between 57 and 48 B.C. in Umbria, perhaps at Assisi. His father was an *eques,* a landowner, and comfortably off. He died while the poet was still a child. In 41 B.C. part of the property Propertius had inherited was confiscated to provide land for the veterans of Antony and Octavian. He began studying for the bar but at an early age abandoned law for poetry. Beyond this we know little. His early years were spent under the shadow of the Civil War that followed the death of Julius Caesar, and this left its marks on his poetry. He was in his late teens or early twenties when Octavian (later Augustus) defeated Antony at the Battle of Actium, and became to all intents sole ruler of the Roman world. His first book (known in antiquity as *Cynthia Monobiblos)* was probably published between 33 and 28 B.C. Maecenas, patron of Horace and Vergil, became his patron. Whether he knew Vergil personally we cannot tell, but he speaks of him with admiration. Relations with Horace appear to have been cool (if the "Callimachus" of Horace Ep. 2.2.91ff is in fact Propertius). Ovid counted him as a friend. We know that he was dead by A.D. 2; the last datable reference in his poems is to 16 B.C. We cannot fix the date of his death more precisely than that.

JOHN WARDEN MAY 1971

SELECT BIBLIOGRAPHY

1. GENERAL DISCUSSIONS

Gordon Williams. *Tradition and Originality in Roman Poetry*. Oxford: Clarendon Press, 1968. Especially Chapter 6 (The Poetry of Institutions); Chapter 7 (Interest in the Individual) section 2; Chapter 8 (Truth and Sincerity); Chapter 10 (Observation, Description and Imagination) section 2; Chapter 11 (Thought and Expression: Language and Style) section 6.

K. Quinn. *Latin Explorations*. London: Routledge & Kegan Paul, 1963. Chapters 6 (Propertius, Horace and the Poet's Role) and 7 (Propertius and the Poetry of the Intellect).

F. O. Copley. Servitium Amoris in the Roman Elegists. *Transactions of the American Philological Association* 78 (1947): 285–300. A discussion of the lover as slave in Roman elegy.

A. W. Allen. Sunt qui Propertium Malint. In *Critical Essays on Roman Literature: Elegy and Lyric*. Ed J. P. Sullivan (Cambridge: Harvard University Press, 1962). An expansion of, "Sincerity" in the Roman Elegists. *Classical Philology* 45 (1950): 145-160.

J. P. Sullivan. *Ezra Pound and Sextus Propertius*. Austin: University of Texas Press. 1964.

———. Propertius, A Preliminary Essay. *Arion* 5 (1966): 5–22.

R. J. Baker. The Military Motif in Propertius. *Latomus* 27 (1968): 322–349.

———. Laus in Amore Mori: Love and Death in Propertius. *Latomus* 29 (1970): 670–698.

A. K. Michels. Death and Two Poets. *Transactions of the American Philological Association* 86 (1955): 160–179. The two poets are Lucretius and Propertius.

Brooks Otis. Propertius' Single Book. *Harvard Studies in Classical Philology* 70 (1965): 1–44. A discussion of the structure of the first book, with some valuable incidental comments on the poet.

Joseph Fontenrose. Propertius and the Roman Career. *University of California Publications in Classical Philology* 13 (1944–50): 371–388.

A. W. Allen. Elegy and the Classical Attitude toward Love: Propertius 1.1. *Yale Classical Studies* 7 (1950): 255–277.

J. P. Sullivan. Castas Odisse Puellas: a Reconsideration of Propertius 1.1. *Wiener Studien* 74 (1961): 96–112.

2. SOME ARTICLES ON INDIVIDUAL POEMS AND GROUPS OF POEMS

L. C. Curran. Vision and Reality in Propertius 1.3. *Yale Classical Studies* 19 (1966): 187–207.

E. W. Leach. Propertius 1.17, the Experimental Voyage. *Yale Classical Studies* 19 (1966): 209–232.

F. Solmsen. Three Elegies of Propertius' First Book. *Classical Philology* 57 (1962): 73–88. The Elegies are 16, 17 and 18.

T. A. Suits. Mythology, Address and Structure in Propertius 2.8. *Transactions of the American Philological Association* 96 (1965): 427–437.

W. R. Nethercut. Ille Parum cauti pectoris egit opus. *Transactions of the American Philological Association* 92 (1961): 389–407.

______. The Ironic Priest. *American Journal of Philology* 91 (1970): 385-407. Both of the above articles look at the first five poems of Book 3.

L. P. Wilkinson. Propertius 3.4. In *Studi in Onore di Luigi Castiglioni,* edited by G. Faranda. Florence: G. C. Sansoni, 1960. (The article is in English.)

W. S. Anderson. Hercules Exclusus: Propertius iv.9. *American Journal of Philology* 85 (1964): 1–12.

3. MORE DETAILED DISCUSSIONS OF PROPERTIUS' LANGUAGE

W. A. Camps. *Propertius: Elegies Book III.* Cambridge: Cambridge University Press, 1966. Introduction pp. 1–8.

J. P. Postgate. *Select Elegies of Propertius.* London: Macmillan, 1884 (and frequently reprinted). Introduction pp. lvii–lxxxviii.

M. W. Edwards. Intensification of Meaning in Propertius and Others. *Transactions of the American Philological Association* 92 (1961): 128–144.

NOTE ON THE TEXT

Propertius' mode of expression makes him a hard poet to interpret at the best of times; and his text is notoriously corrupt. I owe a debt to a long list of scholars: Paley, Postgate, Rothstein, Enk, Butler, Barber, Shackleton Bailey, and, above all, to W. A. Camps for his edition of the poems of Propertius completed in 1967. For the most part I have followed his text, which itself is based on the Oxford text of E. A. Barber.

I am grateful to the editors of *Arion* for permission to reprint two poems, 1.3 and 1.21, which appeared in *Arion* Vol. 4, no. 2.

My thanks to F. O. Copley and to Michael Kirkham for their advice, and to my wife for her criticisms, encouragement, and tolerance.

J.W.

BOOK ONE

CYNTHIA

She was the first to enslave me, and she did it with her eyes;
   till then I'd never felt love's poison arrows.
This time I did—he soon put an end to my haughty looks,
   pinned me down on the floor with his foot on my neck.
He's a harsh tutor—and this is what he's taught me:
   to keep to tarts and live life off the rails.
And now it's been going a year this restless passion,
   with the gods against me all the time.

Milanion managed it—he tamed his proud Atalanta,
   wore down her wildness by never giving up.
He'd roam about in the mountains, half out of his mind,
   stand up to savage beasts with their shaggy coats;
He tackled the lecherous centaur and felt the weight of his club,
   and wounded lay on the rocks, groaning.
That's how he brought that swift-footed girl to heel.
   If you keep on asking and doing your best it works wonders.

But not for me—my love is dull and slow to learn,
   can't even remember the tricks it used to know
Before all this.

You traffickers in magic, who can bring the moon from the sky,
   (or so you say), you, with your rites and altars,
Come show your powers, change the mind of my mistress,
   make her grow pale, yes paler than I am.
Do it and I'll believe your stories of stars and rivers
   drawn from their course by the songs of the Colchian witch.

And you, my friends, who seek to rescue a man far gone,
try to find some cure for a heart that is sick.
I can bear the pain of the surgeon's knife and the savage burning,
so long as I'm free to cry out what my passion bids me.
Take me away to the ends of the earth and beyond the seas,
to a place where woman will never follow.
But do *you* stay at home, whom the god of love favours,
keep your love safe and share it between you.
Just look at me: Venus treats me to nights of torment;
my hopeless passion never leaves me in peace.
This is the state to shun, I tell you; stick to your own love,
each to your own and never seek to change.
And if you forget my words, or leave them till tomorrow,
someday you'll remember them with sorrow.

2

But what's the point, my love

of walking around like a mannequin
with dolled-up hair,
and showing off your sinuous curves
in sheerest silk?

Why do you drench your hair with oils
from Syria
and deck yourself with foreign goods
like a shop window?

You spoil the charms that nature gave
with purchased art.
You have a beauty all your own:
don't hide its light.

You have no need of beauty aids
with such a figure;
love is a naked god and hates
a grace contrived.

The earth is beautiful enough
with her own flowers;
and ivy grows luxuriant
when left alone.

The finest arbute trees spring up
in lonely valleys;
and water knows the way to flow
though never taught.

The pebbles that paint the seashore bright
are all its own;
and birds sing all the sweeter for
their artlessness.

Think of Leucippus' daughters—
They didn't need to paint themselves like you,
    when they made the heavenly twins grow hot.

Nor did Marpessa—
yet she brought a man and a god to blows with her beauty,
    by the banks of her father's watery grave.

Or Hippodamia—
She didn't use any borrowed charms to lure that stranger
    who won her and carried her off with his chariot wheels;
she had a beauty that had no need of precious stones,
    like the colours in a painting by Apelles.

Girls like these didn't walk the streets to look for lovers;
    their modesty was all the beauty they needed.

I know well I mean more to you
than ancient heroes;
and if you please a single lover
that's art enough.

Besides the gods above have blessed you
with many gifts;
friend of the muses you can sing
and play the lyre.

And when you talk your words are witty
and sweet to hear;
all Venus' arts and all Minerva's
they gave to you.

And I shall love you for these charms
throughout my life,
if only you can learn to hate
EXTRAVAGANCE.

3

She looked like Ariadne, lying asleep on her island,
a picture of peace, blind to the parting sail;
Or like Andromeda free at last from her rocky prison,
her limbs relaxed in the first flush of sleep.
She looked like a girl from Thrace played out by her Bacchic dancing,
sunk to rest by the grassy banks of the river.
There she lay, breathing gently, all at peace,
with her head lying on unresisting hands.

Then *I* staggered in, dragging my footsteps, drunk as a lord,
in the small hours, when the torch was burning low.
And I had an urge—I still had *some* of my faculties left—
to tiptoe quietly up to the bed where she lay.
I was growing hot, set on fire by a double flame,
drink and desire, an insistent pair of masters;
Have a go, they said, —put your arms around her softly—
come closer—now then—kiss her—take her by storm.
But I didn't dare disturb her when she looked so quiet and peaceful;
she's a devil when she's roused, as I know too well.
So I just stood there watching, all eyes—like Argus
gazing with some surprise at Io's horns.

And then I took off the garland I still had on from my party,
and put it gently on your sleeping brows.
If your hair was out of place, I lovingly rearranged it,
and smuggled you apples in my cupped hands.
But you were far away—these gifts meant nothing to you,
and they rolled from your lap time and again to the floor.
And once in a while you gave a start and a deep sigh;
I held my breath, quick to believe the worst:

I thought you sighed at a nightmare, full of strange horrors,
  or a man who tried to take you against your will.
And then at last the passing moon shone full in your window,
  the busybody moon, outstaying its welcome.
The pale light of its beams unshuttered your sleeping eyes. . .

  And off she started, propped up in bed on her elbow:
"So you've come at last, and only because that other woman
  has thrown you out and closed the doors against you.
Where have you spent the night—this night that belonged to me?
  Look at you, creeping back with the dawn, a wreck!
It'd do you good to have to spend the sort of night
  you make me spend—you'd learn what cruelty is.
I sat up over my loom, trying to stave off sleep,
  then tired of that and played the lyre a while.
And under my breath I told myself what it's like to be jilted,
  and thought of the hours you spend in another's bed.
Then sleep touched me with soothing wings and brought release;
  but my last thoughts were thoughts of the grief you bring me."

4

Now look here, Bassus,

Do you think that by this catalogue of beauties
   you'll force me to give up my love?
Why won't you let me lead the life I'm born to
   and stick to the devil I know?
You can talk about the fabulous Hermione
   and Antiope, darling of Zeus,
And all the other storybook princesses;
   they can't hold a candle to her.
So it's hardly likely she'd be judged the loser
   if you matched her with ordinary girls.

But it isn't just her figure that inflames me
   and makes all my suffering bliss;
There's more to it than that—her pure complexion,
   those charms she can use to the full,
And all those sweet delights we share together
   in secrecy—under the sheet.
You can't destroy our love—the bonds that join us
   grow stronger the harder you try.

You'll pay for it—when she hears, she'll be furious;
   you'll feel the rough edge of her tongue.
You'll get no visits, no more invitations;
   she'll never forgive you for this.
She'll talk to all her friends and spoil your chances;
   when you call there'll be no one at home.
She'll do the rounds of every shrine and altar
   and call down a curse on your name.
Her lover stolen and her charms left idle—

Oh that's a loss will drive her wild with anger
    worst of all when the lover is me.

God grant that she may always love like this
And never make me doubt her faithfulness.

Oh, stop this endless baiting, you're just jealous;
leave us alone to go our way in peace.

You poor fool, what are you after?
Do you want to feel the savage frenzy I feel?
That's the quick way to plumb the depths of hell,
To drag your footsteps over burning cinders,
and drain the witches' brews of Thessaly.
She isn't like your good-time girls; I'm telling you
when she gets angry, there'll be no half measures.
And even if she gives you what you ask for,
think of the heartache that's in store for you.
She'll invade your dreams and make your eyes her prisoners;
no man's so wild that *she* can't break him in.

And then she'll throw you over. . .
And you'll come running time and again to my doorstep,
and those brave words of yours will end in a whimper;
Shaken with sobs, your nerves all shot to pieces,
your face distorted by the marks of fear,
You'll struggle to find words but stand there tongue-tied,
dazed, like a man who's lost his memory.
Then you'll have to learn what it's like to serve a tyrant
who locks you out and sends you home alone.
It won't surprise you I look pale and sickly,
and my body's worn away to a skeleton.
And don't imagine noble birth will help you;
for love is no respecter of ancestors.
(But give the slightest hint of your attachment,
with a name like yours, you'll be the talk of the town.)

There isn't any comfort I can bring you;
  I haven't found a cure for my own disease.
We'll have each other's shoulders left to weep on,
  sharing our love and sharing our misery.

And so I warn you, Gallus. . .
Stop asking what's so special about Cynthia;
  if you get your way with her, you'll soon find out.

6

It's not that I'm afraid, Tullus,
to join you on a journey across the Adriatic,
   or spread my sails over the Aegean Sea.
With you I would be ready to climb the Scythian mountains,
   or explore the distant lands of Africa.
But Cynthia won't let me go; she puts her arms around me
   and pleads and pleads, her face as white as a sheet.
She keeps it up for nights on end, telling me that she loves me,
   and if I desert her, there's no god in heaven.
She says that I've grown tired of her, flares up at me and taunts me,
   the way girls always do when their man gets cool.
I can't stand up to moods like this; she breaks me down in no time.
   I hate a lover who can keep his head.
Does it mean so much to me to tour the wealthy sites of Asia,
   or visit Athens, cradle of the arts,
That I'd put up with her tantrums, when the ship is at the quayside,
   and bear the marks of her nails on my cheeks?
"I've got the winds to thank," she'll say, "for these last-minute kisses.
   Oh, what's more cruel than a faithless man?"

So you'd better go without me
and set your sights on glories even greater than your uncle's;
   bring peace to those who've forgotten what it means.
For it's always been your passion to fight your country's battles;
   you hadn't any time for love affairs.
And I pray that Cupid spare you the trouble that he's brought me,
   all the suffering and tears I know so well.
But I lie helpless, down and out; so leave me to fate's devices
   to squander my life away, a good for nothing.
There are many who've died happy in a love that lasts a lifetime;
   may I be one of them when I am dust.

I wasn't born for glory, and I'd never make a soldier;
love is the only battle I can fight.
So when you've gone to do your bit for your beloved empire,
whether you journey over land or sea,
Among the soft Ionians, or where Pactolus' water
tinges with gold the fields of Lydia.
If you should ever think of me, you'll know without my telling
that I am still the victim of my fate.

Ponticus, while you write your Theban epic,
how brother fought with brother to the death,
Like a second Homer—and I really mean it—
(if your works should only happen to survive),
As usual it's my love that keeps me busy,
looking for ways to soften a heart of stone.
It's not a poet's skill that makes my verses,
but a broken heart and a lifetime's misery.
That's my life's work and that's my hope of glory;
when they read my verse may people say of me:
No one but he could win a girl so gifted,
or bear the onslaught of her cruel tongue.
In time to come may the deserted lover
read me and learn from my experience.

But when it's your turn to be Cupid's target
(oh may the gods we worship spare you that!)
Your Theban hosts won't hear your cries of anguish;
their deeds will lie forgotten on the shelf.
In vain you'll try to turn your hand to love poems—
when you love so late in life, the words won't come.
And then you'll grant my verses have their merits;
I'll be the greatest poet of them all.
Young men will stand around my grave and murmur:
"O rest in peace, great poet of our love."

So I shouldn't treat my verses with disdain if I were you;
You owe a debt to Cupid, and the interest will accrue.

8

i

Are you crazy, then? I love you. Does that mean nothing to you?
  Am I less to you than Illyria's frozen wastes?
And this fellow you've picked up, do you think him so special
  that you'd sail away and leave me in any weather?
Are you brave enough to stand up to the angry roar of the waves,
  and make your bed on the hard deck of the ship?
Can you bear to trudge through the packed ice with feet so delicate,
  in a land of snow, like nothing you've ever seen?

God grant this year the winter storms last twice as long;
  may the Pleiads come late and keep the sailors idle.
May your ship never weigh anchor, wafted by a following wind,
  a hateful wind, that blows my prayers away.
But when you've gone and the waves are carrying you out to sea,
  then I pray that the winds stay fair for you,
Though you leave me shaking my fist and crying that you are heartless,
  just standing there all alone on the shore;
Whatever you deserve for the cruel way you've treated me,
  may the gods of the sea go with you on your journey,
And guide you safely past Ceraunia's rocky coast,
  and bring you into harbour in calm waters.

You are my love, and no other girl will come between us;
  day after day I'll pour out my grief at your door.
And every sailor I see, I'll call to him and I'll ask him
  "Have you seen her? tell me, where has her ship put in?"
And then I'll say "Let it be in Thessaly, let it be in Scythia,
  What do I care? She shall be mine again."

ii

SHE'S MINE!
Here she is and here she stays;
she gave her word.
My prayers have worn her defences down;
It's victory!

You're out of luck, my jealous friends;
the journey's off!
So stop your wishful thinking now
and go to hell!

The richest kingdom in the world
means nothing to her.
She says that I'm the one she loves,
and I'm in Rome.

If she can share my bed at night
that's all she asks.
So long as she's got me, she'll take
whatever comes.

That's more to her than all the wealth
of Pelop's bride,
the wealth that Elis' horses won
for a line of kings.

Although he gave her many gifts
and promised more,
he couldn't tempt her from my arms
by bribery.

It wasn't gold or precious stones
that swayed her heart;
I won her with the songs of love
I wrote for her.

So never say that there's no power
in poetry;
it's all I had to help my love:
and she's mine again.

SHE'S MINE!

Oh! I'm so happy I could walk
with the gods in heaven.
No one can steal her love from me;
she's mine for good.

And time can't dim the glory of
my victory.

9

Well, Ponticus, I told you so . . .
I said your turn would come, and yet you mocked me;
   I said you'd have to learn to guard your tongue.
Now look at you grovelling, throwing yourself on her mercy
   at the beck and call of a woman who's for sale.
When it comes to saying who's a girl's next victim,
   I'm a better prophet than Dodona's doves;
After all that I've been through I'm quite an expert:
   a distinction that I wish I'd never earned.

What good can Homer do you now?
You'll get no help from tragic tales of heroes,
   or the city walls that rose to Amphion's lyre.
Mimnermus can do more with a single couplet—
   a gentle song to suit a gentle god.
So put those weighty tomes away, I tell you,
   and sing what every woman wants to hear.

You don't know what you're in for yet . . .
You ask for more when your cup is overflowing;
   what would it be like if she wouldn't let you drink?
This is just a spark from the flame that really burns you—
   I can tell by your face that you haven't felt it yet.
And when it comes, you'd rather fight with tigers,
   or join Ixion on the wheel of hell,
Than feel these wounds of love that sap your lifeblood,
   a slave to her every mood, who can't say no.
You never get an easy run from Cupid:
   he gives you your head and then applies the bit.
And if she's willing don't let that deceive you—
   the more she gives herself, the more it hurts:

You won't be allowed to look at another woman
    or ever lose your sleep for someone else.
You'll sample her attractions once too often:
    love shows no symptoms till it's past a cure.
The power of love can conquer trees and mountains;
    there's not much hope for a mere man like you.

So own up while you can, my friend, if you've got any shame;
In a case like yours it often helps if you give the lady's name.

10

What a night that was, when I watched your love's awakening,
   and read your secret in your tears of joy—
A night of bliss, to treasure in the memory,
   a night that I could wish to live again.
I saw you drunk with love in the arms of your sweetheart,
   whispering softly, dwelling on every word.
Though sleep lay heavy on my drowsy eyelids
   (it was getting late and the moon was riding high)
I couldn't bear to leave your tender revels,
   or miss a word from that dialogue of love.

So Gallus, as you weren't afraid to trust me,
   here's a reward for the joys you let me share.
And it isn't just that I can keep a secret;
   My powers go further than mere loyalty.
I can bring together lovers who have parted,
   and open the doors to a girl who's hard to get.
I can soothe your pain, when the wounds are fresh and bleeding;
   you'll find a panacea in my words.
So here are some do's and don't's that Cynthia taught me
   (when you've been in love, you learn a thing or two):
Don't look for trouble when she's feeling moody;
   don't preach her sermons, and don't sit and sulk.
Don't scowl and say no when she asks a favour;
   try to react when she says something nice.
If you treat her with scorn, she'll answer you with fury;
   if you hurt her, you will never live it down.
Forget your pride and tell her you surrender
   if you want to taste love's pleasures to the full.
The only way to be happy with a woman
   is to give her your heart and never want it back.

Baiae,
with its causeway built by Hercules,
and its brand new harbour
that brings the waters of Cape Misenum
under the sway of Avernus . . .

amidst these sights and pleasures, Cynthia,
do you ever lie awake and think of me?
Is there still room for me
somewhere in a corner of your heart?
Or has some stranger with counterfeit passion
erased your name from my verses?

I wish you were on the Lucrine lake
with a little rowing boat to keep you busy,
or safe on Cumae's gently shelving beach,
where the waters don't resist
the swimmer's stroke;
then you wouldn't have time to listen
to these seductive whispers
lying at your ease on the silent beach.

When there's no one to watch her
a girl is easily tempted
to forget the gods and play her lover false.
It's not that I don't trust you—
I know you well enough to know you're faithful;
but no one's love is proof against
a place like this.

So forgive me
if there's anything that offends you in my verses;
it's only my fear that makes me say it.
Don't I look after you more carefully
than my own mother?
and if you leave me
what is there left to live for?
You're everything to me, my life's center
and all the happiness I've ever known.
When I'm sad
and when I'm cheerful
I tell my friends when they ask me why
"ask Cynthia."
Do please come home
and leave those shores before you're led astray.

Baiae,
where many a love affair will founder
and many a respectable girl
has come to grief,
that den of vice
that casts a slur on love itself
I HATE the place.

12

You keep accusing me
of never leaving Rome because my love
belongs to Rome and me.

You haven't got a case:
I tell you she's as many miles away
as Hypanis from the Po.

The things she used to say,
those kisses that gave fuel to my flame,
well that's all over now.

There was a time when I
was dear to her, and I alone could say
that she was true to me.

Was it some jealous god
that laid me low, or was it a magic herb
from the slopes of Caucasus?

What once I was to her
I am no more; for the heart of a girl can change
when she's been away a while.

So I'll have to learn to bear
these lonely nights when I vent my grief aloud
and I'm the audience.

If his girl can see him weep
a man's in luck: for love is not unmoved
by a sacrifice of tears.

65766
LIBRARY
College of St. Francis
JOLIET, ILL.

Or else if he can find
another girl, there's a certain pleasure in
a change of servitude.

But I can never change.
For Cynthia was the first I ever loved,
and she shall be the last.

13

Knowing you, Gallus,
You'll be delighted when you hear what's happened:
I've lost her, and she's left me all alone.
But I'm not going to follow your example—
may you have better luck with—you know who.

You were making quite a name as a gay deceiver
who never stayed too long in the same bed;
But she's done for you at last—I know the symptoms;
at the first step on the slippery slope, you fell.
She'll see those girls you slighted get their own back,
she'll make you pay for all those broken hearts;
Gone are the days when you could be free with your favours:
You'll find you've lost your appetite for change.

Now I'm no prophet and I haven't been listening to scandal;
will you contradict what I saw with my own eyes?
You couldn't keep your hands off her—I saw you
locked in her arms in an ecstasy of love,
Dying to touch those lovely lips—the details
my modesty forbids me to reveal.
You were driven out of your minds by a storm of passion
that bound you so fast I couldn't tear you apart.

Think of Neptune:
He didn't feel like this when he got his way with Tyro
by merging himself with the river that she loved.
Or Hercules:
Lying on Oeta all ablaze—with love for Hebe,
when he tasted the first pleasures of being a god.

In a single day of loving you've outstripped them all;
  for the torch that set you on fire was blazing hot.
So say good-bye to your cavalier ways—she's going to keep you:
  this passion of yours will lead you quite a dance.

But I don't blame you . . .
She'd hold her own with all those ancient beauties,
  if Jupiter were looking for a mate—
Except for Leda—but as for Leda's children
  she's got more charm than all of them put together.
She knows how to make the most of her attractions;
  why, she could *talk* him into loving her.

A love like this comes only once in a lifetime;
  so take your chance—she's just the girl for you.
And I pray she may be all that you could wish for,
  and bring you joy in your new experience.

14

You can keep your large estate
with its lofty groves like the woods of Caucasus
towering towards the sky:

Where you lie on Tiber's bank
taking your ease and sipping your Lesbian wine
from a cup that Mentor made,

and watch the boats go by,
the little skiff that darts across the surface
and the slow-moving barge.

For love can conquer wealth
and all your luxury can never match
the splendour of my love.

Those nights of ecstasy
those days of sweet delight I spend with her
are wealth enough for me:

Pearls from Arabian seas
and treasures from Pactolus' golden stream
come flowing to my door.

O may this happiness
that makes me richer than the richest king
be mine until I die.

May it never be my fate
to win a fortune and to lose my love;
for Venus can be cruel.

No man is strong enough
to stand against her, and no heart too dull
to feel her agony.

You can't escape from her
behind an onyx threshold or beneath
a purple coverlet.

As you toss and turn all night
you'll find no comfort for the pangs of love
in a silken canopy.

But I can laugh to scorn
the wealth of King Alcinous himself
with Venus on my side.

15 

You can be cruel
(I've learnt to fear your fickleness)
but I never thought you'd go as far as this.

For you can see
what dangers lie in store for me;
but when I need you most you take your time.

You sit for hours
touching up yesterday's coiffure
and painting your face in front of a looking glass,

Dressing to kill
your breast bespangled with precious stones
like a girl who's going to meet a new lover.

Think how Calypso wept when she'd said good-bye to Ulysses
all alone with her grief on the seashore;
She sat there for days on end, rebuking the cruel waves,
too much in love to care what her hair looked like.
When she remembered the hours of joy they'd spent together
she wished him safe—and *he* was gone for good.

And think what Hypsipyle felt for her guest from Haemon's banks
when he sailed away on the winds and broke her heart;
She shut herself up in her bedroom, that seemed so empty now,
and never again tasted the joys of love.

Evadne found her end on her husband's funeral pyre,
and gave the Greeks a name for chastity.

And Alphesiboea's love broke through the ties of blood,
when her brothers paid with death for the death of her husband.

But *you* won't change your ways—no stories of ancient heroines
could ever make a legend out of you.

You swear you love me
with oaths that you've already broken;
do you want to jog the memory of the gods?

Don't take such chances;
for if you're made to suffer for it,
remember I'm the one it really hurts.

Do you think that rivers
could ever flow backwards from the ocean,
or the seasons of the year go topsy-turvy?

Do you think my heart
could ever lose its love for you?
Oh treat me how you like, but never leave me.

Those eyes of yours
that only had to look at me
and I would fall for every word you said

Are they so cheap
that you could pledge the gods with them
to strike you blind if you have told a lie?

And do you dare
to look in the face of the mighty sun?
Do you think he doesn't know your guilty secret?

You hypocrite
you didn't have to go so pale
and force your eyes to weep against their will.

The moral is:
the more a woman tries to charm you
the more you'll keep your distance if you're wise

So speaks the victim of a pair of eyes.

16

Once I was a famous door,
the guardian of virginity;
but I'm not famous any more.

Where once triumphal chariots
thronged in solemn pageantry
there's nothing now but drunken sots;

Where captive suppliants used to weep,
they shout and brawl and beat me up
when decent people are asleep.

And cast-off garlands decorate
my portals, and the burnt-out torch
that shows a man he's come too late.

My mistress doesn't seem to care
though she's the loosest girl in Rome,
and you know what modern Romans are.

And *I* can't stop her doing wrong.
Alas that I should come to this:
the subject of a dirty song.

And then, what makes it even worse,
there's always someone left outside
who tries to woo me with his verse;

He never lets me sleep in peace
but pesters me the whole night through
with shrill laments that go like this:

"O cruel, cruel door, more heartless than my mistress,
  will you never open up and let me in?
Will nothing ever move you to break your stubborn silence
  and smuggle in a message to my love?
Or will I have to spend the night in this unhappy vigil,
  and use your draughty threshold as a bed?

Look, even nature pities me, the stars high in their courses,
  the midnight hours, the chilly breeze of dawn.
But you alone are pitiless, unmoved by mortal suffering;
  your hinges never creak in sympathy.
A tiny chink is all I ask, through which my voice could enter
  and find its way to her pretty little ears;
For though the rocks of Aetna were never so unyielding,
  and her heart were harder than the hardest steel,
Her eyes would weep in spite of her, if she could hear my singing,
  and sighs of love would mingle with her tears.
But now a luckier man than I has got his arms around her,
  and my words are blown away on the winds of night.

It's you, ungrateful door, it's you that makes me suffer;
  and yet I've always tried to treat you well:
I've tried not to offend you by being disrespectful,
  or making vulgar jokes at your expense.
So why do you make me spend the night in torment on the pavement,
  and plead for sympathy until I'm hoarse?
Haven't I knelt upon your steps and smothered them with kisses
  and sung you songs you've never heard before?
Think of the times I've prayed to you and brought you secret offerings.
  O faithless door, how could you be so cruel?"

And so with such familiar words
that every jilted lover knows
he tries to drown the morning birds.

And now I'm a notorious door,
the guardian of her infamy;
and no one likes me any more.

I'm all alone
with only the halcyons to talk to;
Cassiope
will never again look upon my ship
and bring me to safety;
the cruel shore
is deaf to all my prayers.

And yet it serves me right

because I dared to leave her.

Cynthia
listen, can't you hear
the wild storm's raging?
The elements your representatives
are doing your work for you.
Will my luck never change
and the winds be at peace?
Or must I make my grave here
with nothing to cover my body
but a few grains of sand?

Cynthia forgive me
soften your savage anger;
the sky is dark with storm clouds
treacherous rocks lurk in the shallows:
haven't I been punished enough?
When you're going to my funeral
cradling an empty urn
won't you be sorry then?

A curse on him
whoever he was
who first built a sailing boat
and forced a passage over the unwilling sea.

I scan the woods that fringe the shore
but find no signs of life
and wait in vain for the Twins
to flash the light that sailors long for.
Why didn't I stay at home
(she couldn't be more cruel than this)
and learn to be the master of her moods
and of her beauty?

If death had come to me there
and put my sorrow in the grave
with a stone to mark a lover's resting place,
her gentle hands
would have laid my bones on soft rose-leaves
her precious hair
would have been my parting gift
her voice
would have called my name in a last farewell
and the earth would not lie heavy on me.

O nymphs of the sea
children of lovely Doris
guide my ship with your propitious dance
let the white sails swell.

If ever the god of love
has swooped like a bird from the sky
and lighted on your waves,
pity a fellow sufferer
and bring me safe to shore.

18 

This place seems lonely enough
for a man to weep without fear of interruption;
only the breath of the wind
fills the empty grove.

No one can stop me here
from broadcasting the secret of my grief
providing the desolate rocks
don't turn informer.

Where shall I start
this tale of your contempt?
Cynthia, tell me, what can you provide
as a proem to my tears?

—To think they used to call me lucky in love;
and now my love for you
has marked me down a failure.

What had I done?
What is the charge against me
that I deserved to lose your love
as punishment

—another woman?

I swear to you
that as I hope that you'll come back to me
I've never played host to anyone else's beauty.
Though I've a debt of suffering to pay you

I'm not so cruel
that I could give you substance for your fury
and make you spoil your lovely eyes with weeping.

—that you couldn't see my feelings
written on my face
and didn't hear me
shouting aloud to the world that I'd be true?

I call the trees to witness
the birch tree
(she's been in love)
and the pine tree darling of Pan.
Under their gentle shade
rang out my words of passion,
and the name I carved in their bark
was CYNTHIA.

—that your cruel treatment
had given a voice to my unhappiness
though I kept it a secret
between me and your front door?

By force of habit
I've learnt to be a coward;
I bow to your imperious commands
and keep my suffering to myself.

And what is my reward?
These icy mountain-crags,
this wild deserted track,
the unfeeling silence.

Here I'll have to stay
and tell the story of my misery

with no one to hear me
but the shrill-tongued birds.

But treat me how you will,
I'll make the forest echo to your name
and the lonely rocks
cry "CYNTHIA."

19

I do not fear death
or the grim shades of hell;
what do I care
that the funeral pyre
must claim its own at last?
But more than death
and all its trappings
I fear to die unloved.

Beyond the grave
I'll still remember;
for Cupid struck me through the eyes
and the wound sank deep.

Down there
in the world of darkness
Protesilaus couldn't forget
his darling Laodamia.
Back he came a ghost
to his old Thessalian home
and sought to grasp the joys he used to know
with insubstantial hands.

And when I join the shades
down there
whatever's left of me
will still belong to you.
For love is strong
and leaps the shores of death.

Let the beauties of the dead,
Troy's gift of plunder to the Greeks,
perform their dance.
Yet none of them will seem to me
more beautiful than you.

And though death keeps you waiting
till you are old
(O Earth be just
and grant this prayer)
yet shall I greet your ashes with my love
and with my tears.

Grant me such love, such tears
while you still live
and I am in the tomb,
and death will lose its bitterness
even in the depths of hell.

But how I fear
my tomb will be forgotten
my bones forsaken
when some unscrupulous lover
makes you dry your tears against your will;
for woman's loyalty will yield
to man's insistence.

So let us share our love
and our delight
while there is time;
for lover's time
is all too short.

20

Gallus, as you love me well
mark my words, and don't forget
the cautionary tale I tell.

Lake Ascanius reports
that careless lovers come to grief;
he proved it to the Argonauts.

They tell me that your latest flame
is a second Hylas in his looks
and not dissimilar in name.

So if you take him for a row
along Clitumnus' shady streams
or paddling in the Anio,

Or stroll with him on Baiae's coast,
or any place you visit where
a wandering river is your host,

Watch out for nymphs, and keep him free
from all their amorous attacks
(they're just as bad in Italy).

Or else you'll have to do a tour
of barren mountains, icy cliffs
and lakes you've never seen before.

Hercules once suffered thus:
in tears he tramped the unknown shores
but couldn't sway Ascanius.

The story goes that the Argo was well on its way to Colchis,
with the docks of Pagasae left far behind;
It glided past the waters of the Hellespont
and came to rest on the rocks of Mysia;
Once it had moored in a sheltered haven, the crew of heroes
laid soft beds of leaves along the shore.
But Hylas had gone further afield to look for water
from distant springs—for water there was scarce.
After him went the two sons of the North Wind,
Zetes and Calais, hovering over their prey;
In turns they swooped with arms outstretched to snatch a kiss,
then wheeled aloft and bore away the prize.
He leaned forward, shielding his face behind his arm,
and beat off the airborne ambush with a branch.
At length they gave up the chase—and Hylas went his way,
he went his way to the dryads—and disaster.
There's a spring that lies beneath the peak of mount Arganthus,
the favourite haunt of Thynian water-nymphs;
And up above it apples, the fruit of no man's labour,
hang wet with dew on long-forgotten trees;
And round about it lilies grow in the water-meadows
with poppies intermingled, red with white.
The sight of the flowers made the boy forget the task he'd come for;
and he stopped to pluck them with his delicate fingers;
Then whiled away the time, lying at the water's edge,
gazing spellbound at his mirrored beauty.
To work at last: leaning his weight on his right shoulder,
he lowered his urn and filled it to the brim.
Dazzled by his loveliness, the nymphs gave up their dancing;
hot with desire, they gathered round in wonder.
Forward he fell, lightly drawn through the yielding waters;
he gave a cry for help—and then was gone.
Far off Alcides called and called—but the only answer
was an echo borne on the winds from the distant spring.

So Gallus learn to guard your love
and don't entrust him to the nymphs:
for it rather looks as though you have.

PROPERTIUS

21

"Soldier
fleeing wounded from the Tuscan ramparts
to avoid a fate like mine,
why do you stare like that
and roll your eyes in horror at my groaning?
For I was one of you,
your comrade.

Save yourself
and bring your parents joy,
but to my sister Acca
a message in your tears
That I, Gallus, escaped from the swords of Caesar
only to die at the hands of robbers.

And of all the bones
that lie scattered over the Tuscan hills
tell her that these are mine."

22

You ask me, Tullus, in the name of our long friendship,
where do I come from, what are my household gods.
You know Perugia, don't you—
that graveyard of our fatherland
when civil war set Roman against Roman
and Italy suffered
(but none so much as I—
O Tuscan soil
my kinsman's bones lie scattered on your hillside,
and you haven't thought to give them burial)
not far from there
where the fertile plain touches the foothills
Umbria gave me birth.

BOOK TWO

1

i

Question:
where are they from, these songs of love that crowd my pages
        and make their yielding way to the lips of men?
I am the mouthpiece for no muse or god:
SHE
is the whole of my inspiration
Dress her in shimmering silk and make her walk—
        and that's the stuff of a whole volume;
or say I see her with her hair down, tumbling all over her brow:
        I write a hymn to hair, and she's happy as a queen.
If she strikes music from the lyre with delicate fingertips,
        I sing my wonder for her casual art;
or when those eyes of hers droop at sleep's prompting,
        why there's a thousand brand new themes for poetry.
Naked
    (I've stripped her of her cloak)
                                        and locked with me in single combat
    Oh whole epics were written for less.
It doesn't matter what she does or what she says
        each trivial incident begets
        a mighty saga.

ii

But just suppose, Maecenas,
the fates had granted me the power
to muster bands of heroes and march them into battle,
I would avoid the following topics:
—Titans

—Ossa on O-
lympus piled
so Pelion might be
an access route to heaven
—Ancient Thebes, and Troy, synonymous with Homer
—Twin waters wedded by command of Xerxes
—The infant realm of Remus and the pride of lofty Carthage
—Cimbrian aggression and the achievements of Marius
—etc.

Your Caesar's wars and works and you to mighty Caesar
second would be the subject of my song.
If I should tell of Mutina
or Philippi Rome's common graveyard
or the naval wars and routs of Sicily;
of the ancient homesteads of Etruscans sacked
or Alexandria captured and the Nile
dragged impotent through the city
its sevenfold streams in chains;
of golden halters on the necks of kings,
and the prows of Actium breasting the Sacred Way
Your name would run like a thread through my verses
true fellow-combatant in peace and war.
Such loyalty as yours
Theseus and Achilles would recognise;
They'd pledge to it Patroclus and Pirithous.

iii

Don't ask for thunder from Callimachus
for the clash of gods and giants on Phlegra's plain—
He hasn't got the lungs; nor I the heart
for tracing Caesar's family tree to its Phrygian roots
in tough verses.
Each man should stick to what he's best at:
The ploughman talks of his bulls,

The sailor sings of the deep,
The soldier tells of his battle scars,
And the shepherd talks of his sheep.
Master of a narrow field I sing instead
of the battles I fight in bed.

iv

Dulce et decorum est
to die for love
second best
to have but one—O may she be all mine to have.
She often says (if I remember rightly)
she has not time for flighty girls
(if I remember rightly)
She just can't take the Iliad at all
because of that Helen.
And as for me the potions of a Phaedra
would leave me as cold as Hippolytus;
though I should feed on Circe's herbs
or bubble in Medea's pot
she, she alone will send my body on its last journey
for she has stolen away my heart.

There is a cure for every human ill—save one
love has no love for the healer's craft.
examples: a) Philoctetes
lame
b) Phoenix
blind
c) Androgeon
dead
restored to his father's halls
by a recipe of home-grown simples
from the healing god himself
d) Telephus
brought relief by the very weapon

that dealt the wound.
No, not even that; there is no cure for my sickness.
You might as well press apples into Tantalus' hands,
fetch water for the Danaids in a leaky urn
(don't let that burden chafe their tender skin forever),
set free Prometheus shackled to his Caucasian rock,
and beat off the bird that rummages in his vitals.

So when my span is done and the fates claim my life
and I become a little name on an obscure tomb,
Maecenas, hope and envy of our youth,
part of whose lustre falls on me,
in death as in life,
if you should chance to pass close to my tomb,
rein in your chariot,
that fashionable model with its carved yoke,
let drop a tear and speak out to my unresponding ashes
something like this:
HERE LIES ONE FOR WHOM DESTINY
WAS A CRUEL MISTRESS.

2

Freedom I thought and dreamed of a life
with a bed to call my own
I signed a treaty with love—but love
welshed, and the dream was gone.

If beauty like this still lingers on among mortals
how can you blame Jupiter
for past indiscretions?
Golden hair,
elegant fingers,
a full body,
and she walks like the queen of heaven
or Pallas Athene striding before her altars
holding the snake-haired Gorgon at her breast.
She makes me think of Lapith Ischomache
the Centaurs' sweet spoils
just what they needed to go with their wine;
or Brimo who they say
by the banks of lake Boebe
offered her virgin body to the god.
Give way you goddesses
who once on Mount Ida
stood naked before a shepherd's scrutiny.
Beauty like this
may the years not mar
though she lives to the Sibyl's age.

3

Woman-proof, eh?
Proud words but just look at you:
Barely a month's rest
and another shameful volume
ready for writing.

It was an experiment
to find out whether fishes
could live on the dry land
or the savage boar
change his natural habitat
in favour of the ocean
or Propertius
take to serious study
and work nights.

But you can't get away from love
he breaks you down
in his own good time.
It wasn't so much her beauty (Oh, her beauty—
skin whiter than lilies
Spanish vermilion set against snows of Tauris
rose petals floating on milk)
or her hair flowing modishly
over her delicate shoulders
or her eyes burning like torches
twin stars of my firmament;
and any girl can glow
with the sheen of Arabian silk
(I'm not the sort
to fall for things like that)

But the way she dances
(when dinner's over and the wine is served)
graceful as Ariadne queen among maenads
and plays the lyre with the skill of the muse herself
and writes like a second Corinna
Oh my darling
on the day that you were born
shining love
sneezed loud and clear
and all the other gods heaped on you
presents from heaven
(not as you may think
your mother's womb; gifts like yours
are products of no human parturition
nine months is far too short)

Glory to Rome and her daughters at your birth
first among women
Never before has Jupiter
offered his bed to a Roman
But you are not destined forever
to sleep with a human
Helen has gone—but beauty has returned
No wonder youth's ablaze
for you Troy would have burned
in a lovelier cause
Paris and Menelaus you were right
to demand and to refuse
Beauty's a fit excuse
For Achilles to die and Priam to fight
Europe and Asia clash in armed might:
I understand the origin of wars.
Artists, here's a model
the old masters couldn't match:
paint a picture of my darling
show it westward show it eastward
East and West will burst in flames.

So now I know my place, and may I learn to keep it
(I'd rather die than fall in love again)
and imitate the bull
who after his first proud resistance
goes placid to the plough beneath the well-known yoke;
So hot young men when first in love
will baulk and shy
but later when they're broken in
they learn to take the rough with the smooth.
Melampus though a seer
was thrown in jail for cattle theft
and all he stood to gain
was the hand of lovely Pero.

You'll curse her faithlessness, and get
no answer when you call;
you'll tap your angry foot and gnaw
your innocent fingernail.
Though you walk with a slow swagger
and drench your hair with oil—
it's all to no avail.

No use in herbs or simples brewed
in Perimede's pot;
No viruses or broken bones
on the medical report;
Where the pains come from no one knows—
but still they hurt.

No need to call the doctor
no need to rest in bed;
there's nothing wrong with the climate,
and it's not that the air is bad;
You're walking around one day—and then
you drop down dead.

I've had my dreams turned inside out;
I've paid consulting fees
to every prophet-quack in town;
but all I've learnt is this,
that love is unpredictable,
whatever else it is.

I offer to my enemies
such heterosexual joys

and to my friends some good advice:
  find your delight in boys.

Sail your boat on a quiet stream,
  where the waters gently lap;
when boys are mad a single word
  will often make them stop;
but she will have your very blood
  to the last drop.

5

Listen to what they say:
Cynthia the city whore
all Rome's her beat.
Is it true? could you do that? you'll pay for it you traitor;
I too can set my sail to another breeze.
Somewhere
among the fickle ranks of women
there must be one
(my poems are good publicity)
who'll not treat me as the butt
of her callous caprices.
She'll sting you to remember
how long I loved you;
and you'll weep—but weep too late.

NOW
now is the time to quit while your anger's still hot;
when you start to feel the pain, that's love returning.
A single word to a lover—and all his fury
passes like a squall on the Carpathian Sea
or the black storm clouds, when a southerly unsettles the weather
Now's your chance, just slip the yoke and you're a free man.
It'll hurt a little at first—that empty bed on the first night;
but time dulls the pain, if you can bear it.

Oh Cynthia
tell me by Juno mistress of our common bondage
whose tender sacraments we shared
why must you hurt yourself like this my darling?
I'll grant I am no bull
to charge and toss my foe on crooked horn,

but wounded and at bay
even a sheep fights back.
There'll be no vulgar brawling—
I'll not strip naked your cheating body

nor break down the door that will not let me in

nor grab in anger at your braided hair

nor bruise you (god forbid) with rough fists;

I am a poet—not a peasant.
And so I'll write a poem
which will mark you till your dying day;
scorn as you will
the mutterings of reputation
these words will make you blench:

IN BEAUTY CYNTHIA EXCELS
(but you should hear the lies she tells).

6

No ancient beauty had a house
as full of men as yours;
Not Thais though the whole of Greece
was beating at her doors;
or Lais who from Menander won
the title of a play,
and for the sons of Erichthon
became the people's toy;
"what Alexander has destroyed
shall be restored by Phryne":
so many lovers she enjoyed
with such a lot of money—
but you have twice as many.

You've got me in a state of nerves,
a prey to jealous guesses.
Do you invent those relatives
to legalise your kisses?
A young man's picture in a frame
will fill me with alarms,
the very mention of a name,
even a babe in arms,
if it's a boy; and when I see
you and your mother kissing,
or your sister or a girl maybe
who shares your bed, suspicion
makes every little gesture hurt
(forgive me if you can);
I fear that under every skirt
there lurks a man.

Sex can lead to violence
        for sex they say Troy fell,
and the Centaurs raised their heavy cups
        and crushed Pirithous' skull.
Brought up tough on the pap of a wolf
        (an example nearer home)
you founded our city, Romulus,
        thanks to a sex crime;
when there were virgins to be raped
        you coached the team;
and thereby set the present trend
        of sexual life in Rome:
any girl who's glad to be
        behind her husband's door
is blessed as Penelope
        and just about as rare;
the temples built to chastity
        aren't needed any more.

Look at those dirty pictures
        that decorate your wall;
whoever was the first to dare
        such secrets to unveil
and share his own depravity
        with some unsuspecting girl,
a curse on him! such mystic joys
        should never see the light,
concealed beneath the knowledge of
        unspeakable delight.
In times gone by no painted walls
        bore witness to such deeds:
now spiders deck the temples and
        the gods are rank with weeds.

No doors will keep the enemy out,
        no grim-faced janitor;
a girl, unless she wants to be,
        can never be secure;

and yet she's safe enough in bed
if her intention's pure.

But as for me I'll never give
my heart to wife or lover;
Cynthia is my only love,
my only wife forever.

You were happy, Cynthia, weren't you, when you heard they'd dropped the bill
Oh the tears we shed when it was introduced.
Yet what had we to fear? what love has joined together,
even Jupiter himself can't put asunder.
But what of mighty Caesar, the conqueror of nations?
Well, mighty Caesar cannot conquer love.

I'd rather have this head of mine severed from my shoulders
than waste a lover's torches on a bride;
imagine me in procession passing by your doorway,
turning my head and weeping for what I've lost;
and you hearing in your sleep the flute's serenading,
a sound more doleful than the funeral trump.

Anyway how can *I* breed heroes for my country?
no son of mine could ever be a soldier.
But if I went campaigning under my sweetheart's banner,
I'd need a mount more spirited than Castor's.
That's real soldiering for you, and the glory of my exploits
reaches the frozen sons of Olbia.

Cynthia, you are my only love; may you have no other;
and that means more to me than the name of father.

8 

They've taken away the girl I love;
                and you bid me shed no tear.
But a lover hates his rival
                more than his own murderer.
Am I supposed to stand and watch
                as she lies in another man's arms?
And hear what once was mine
                called by other men's names?

Sceptre and crown etc.—
                that's what they say;
Thebes lies in the dust
                and Troy has had its day.
The cliche's true
                for love at any rate—
victor and vanquished change places
                in love's roundabout.

The songs I wrote for her, the presents I gave her
couldn't make her say just once "I love you."

        What do you think I am?
            your domestic servant?
        Fool that I was for so many years
        to do my household duties
        and bear the lash of milady's tongue.

                You're young to die, Propertius—
                but die you must—and may she exult in it,
                let her hound my shade and persecute my spirit,

trample on my pyre and grind my bones to powder.
On Antigone's tomb Haemon
sank his sword deep in his own body
mingled his bones with the bones of his loved one
and wouldn't go home alone.

No more will you—you too must die;
the blood that drips from my sword
shall not be mine alone.
And yet your death will bring me shame.
Well, shame me then—but die.

Achilles when they took away his beloved
stayed in his tent alone,
he watched the Achaeans strewn in flight along the shore,
he watched the Greek ships burn,
he saw Patroclus stretched out dead
mudspattered, his hair bloodied and torn—
and all for his lovely Briseis:
so great was his anger at his love's loss

and when they gave her back at long last
he dragged the mighty Hector in the dust.

Now I'm no hero and my mother wasn't a goddess;
Love leads me captive; so how can I resist?

9a

What he is now
I was
and when his time is up
another will be.

Penelope for twenty years
preserved herself intact
and proved herself worthy of her many wooers,
staving off marriage with a trick of the loom
nightly unravelling her daytime's weaving;
she never thought to see Ulysses again
but she waited for him—and grew old in the waiting.

Briseis
embraced Achilles dead
and tore at her lovely face with crazed hands;
in grief she washed away the blood from the body of her lord and master
laid out for all to see by Simois' golden waters.
She it was who mourned at his pyre
(not Peleus
nor his mother who lives in the sea
nor his widow Deidamia).
She fouled her hair with dust, and when it was over
lifted in her tiny hand
all that was left of that massive frame.
And Greece rejoiced at one who was a true wife
though but a prize of war
blessed in her faithfulness
even on the field of battle.

But you, you godless traitor
you couldn't hold off for a single night
or spend one day alone.
There you were, drinking and laughing the hours away
(with jokes, I'll bet, at my expense).
and the one you're after, he's already left you once
(God grant you catch him—and I wish you joy of it).
When I was praying for you to be well again
and the Stygian waters swirled about your head,
and we stood by your sickbed—a group of friends weeping,
where was he then, tell me that, what was he to you?
All in a single day; suppose I were kept away from home
campaigning in the distant Indies
or becalmed in the middle of the ocean
what then?

Lies and deceit come easily to women;
in this craft they're all experts.
You know how the sandshoals shift when the winds are changing
how the leaves are all aquiver when a gale blows from the south;
they are less fickle than a woman's whim
who breaks her word for any cause or none.

Still if that's the way you want it, so be it.
And I pray you Cupids, choose out your sharpest arrows,
make me the target of your shooting match (first prize: my life)
shoot me dead and let me go.
Let the stars bear witness and the frosts of dawn and the door
    that opened just a chink to let me in
that you have always been dearer to me than the whole world,
    and though you hate me, will be always dear.
My bed will never bear the prints of another woman's body;
    if I cannot belong to you, I'll belong to no one.
And if I have lived a life of piety, may the gods grant
    that as you lie together in the act of love
        that man be turned to stone.

As once Jocasta watched
as brother slew brother in grim conflict
for the sake of a kingdom
so I would fight you to the death
  my death for yours
if Cynthia were watching.

10

Enough:
it is time to dance a holier dance on Helicon
    and let my charger range the open plain.
My Caesar's Roman hosts
his squadrons bold to the fray
I choose as subject now.
And if I have not strength to sing so great a theme
it is enough to have wanted to;
to dare to try and fail
is glory in itself.
My song shall be of war and war's alarms:
love is a young man's matter
and Cynthia's song is sung.
Now I am minded to walk more stately, stern of brow
now my Muse will teach me
another style of playing:

"Take wings, my soul, ye songs, put on more strength,
    Pierian maids give power to your voices!
Hearken Augustus, to the tale Euphrates tells:
no longer do the Parthian horsemen swivel in the saddle;
    they have learnt to rue the standards of the Crassi.
And India bends her neck to your triumphal car
    and the virgin house of Arabia trembles.
That land, if land there be, that cowers at the world's edge,
    may she too feel the weight of your conquering hand."

These shall be my standards
I shall grow famous as the laureate of your exploits
(god grant I see the day).

But when a statue towers too high
its head beyond reach
one lays the wreath before its feet;
so I whose meagre art
cannot mount high enough in song
to sing your praises
worship as a poor man does—with frankincense.
For I have not yet drunk of Hesiod's spring;
my songs are bathed in a lowlier stream
            by the hand of love.

11

My songs of love are written
find someone else
or be forgotten

The one who praises you
sows his seed
where no crops grow

Remember this
when the dark day comes
and your life is at its close

Your beauty and your gifts
will die with you
and there'll be nothing left

No traveller passing by
will spare your tomb a glance
or stop and say

"This girl had beauty wit and elegance."

12

i

He was a genius who painted love
as a little child; he understood how lovers
squander their fortunes on a worthless toy
and live as children do without caring;

He gave him wings, lighter than the wind,
a god in the hearts of men to hover:
(so we are buffeted from wave to wave,
and the breath of love is always veering)

He put barbed arrows in his hand
and on his back a Cretan quiver:
(we fear no danger till the sniper strikes;
and once struck, the wound's past curing)

ii

I recognise the childish face
the arrows too are all in place
    only the wings are missing
for love has lost the power of flight
and stays forever in my heart
    and wages war unceasing

Leave me alone, you've sucked me dry
the one you torture is not I
    but just an empty shell

go find yourself a virgin heart
that has not felt your poison dart
  a better place to dwell

Remember if I die you'll lose
great glory from my slender muse
  for who will then be left
to hymn my love from top to toe
and sing of how her dark eyes glow
  and how she walks so soft?

13a

Love who has plugged my heart more full of arrows
than a Persian armoury
bids me respect my muse and make her delicate charms
at home in Hesiod's grove;
not seeking to draw oak trees in my train
or lead wild animals through the vales of Thrace
but to bind Cynthia with my spell—
so would my art outstrip the glory of Linus

I ask for something more than a beautiful figure
and a fine pedigree
a girl with the wit to listen to my songs of love
as she holds me in her arms;
judged by a critic with an ear so fine
I'll let the scandal-mongers go to hell—
Oh if she'll bend her ear to peace
what do I care if Jupiter's my enemy?

13b

Against the day when death shall close my eyes
here are my funeral instructions:
I want no long parade
of ancestors in solemn file
no trumpet keening pointlessly
no ivory footrest to my bier
no cloth of gold to prop my corpse
no perfumed platters in a row

but a simple ceremony without expense
as my cortege
my books of verse
(the best I have to offer
to the queen of the dead)
and you behind my bier
tearing your naked breasts
and over and over calling out my name.
When the time comes
open the jar of alabaster
pour out your offering of Syrian nard
and kiss my lips
now cold in death
for the last time.
Then set me alight and let me burn.
Let a small earthen pot
contain my ashes
and on my humble tomb
may a laurel grow
to shade the place where my dead embers lie.
and add these lines as epitaph:

The hideous remains
        that lie beneath this stone
once served the god of love—
        and loved but one.
So shall my tomb wax in glory like the tomb of Achilles
stained with a virgin's blood.

And don't forget the way;
and when it's time for you to make your journey
come white with age to join me here
for the tomb does not forget.
And while you live I'm warning you
don't treat my ashes with dishonour
there is a sentience among the dead
        they know your secrets.

I wish that some convenient fate
had bid me breathe my last
as I lay in my cradle
For why do we so jealously guard
this fleeting moment of precarious life?
Nestor took three generations to die;
if some rough Trojan in the trenches
had shortened his longevity
he would never have had to say
as he watched his son's corpse lowered in the earth
Death have you forgotten me?

And sometimes then you'll weep for me
your dear departed:
you have to love a lover when he's dead.
They say that when Adonis
went hunting on the peaks of Ida
and the brutal boar ripped his snow white skin
Venus went to her lover
and washed his shapely body in the marshy pools,
with her hair streaming free.

But it's too late to call me then Cynthia;
for the grave is silent:
what answer can you get from crumbling bones?

14a

Imagine Agamemnon's joy
when he stood and looked on conquered Troy
as the wealth and power of generations fell;

Ulysses standing on the shore
at last a wanderer no more
rejoiced to touch the land he loved so well;

How gladly did Electra learn
she'd shed her tears for an empty urn
when she saw her brother who she thought was dead;

In bliss did Ariadne gaze
on Theseus safe back from the maze
his footsteps guided by a little thread:

But no such mythical delight
can match the joys I knew last night;
another night like that and I'll be a god.

*

I used to meet with haughty quips:
"I never drink from public taps—
especially when the reservoir is dry;"

that's when I went to her on my knees:
this time she didn't sit at ease,
and coolly hear my plea and say good-bye.

These are the rules—it's nice to know
(I wish I'd learnt them long ago;
you don't give drugs when the patient's in his grave);

The path shone bright before my eyes;
but I was blind (that's no surprise:
for nobody can see when he's mad with love);

So here's my recipe for success:
treat her with scorn and she'll soon say yes—
what yesterday she refused today she'll give.

*

Outside they beat the door in vain
and called her "mistress"; she was mine.
Languid she lay contented at my side.

This triumph is more real to me
than any Parthian victory;
these are my spoils and this my victory ride.

Rich gifts in Venus' shrine I'll hang
and dedicate this little song,
and sign my name, as an offering of thanksgiving:

GODDESS, THESE VICTORY SPOILS ARE YOURS:
PROPERTIUS LAYS THEM AT YOUR DOORS
IN GRATITUDE FOR A WHOLE NIGHT OF LOVING.

14b

It's up to you my darling
whether my laden ship has come to rest
    safe on the shore
    or grounded in the shallows;
if anything makes you change towards me now
you'll find me lying on your threshold
                                                        dead.

15

O MY DREAM COME TRUE

O shining night
O bed by the sweets of my darling
        sanctified

First we talked in the lamplight then
        when the lights were out
            the donnybrook
One moment breasts naked she wrestled me
then pulled her tunic to
                                and made me wait
And when my eyelids drooped in sleep
with her mouth she kissed them open and said
        "Don't just lie there . . .
                                        slowcoach . . ."
O the tangle of arms clasping, O the kisses
when you held me with your lips and wouldn't let go.

But why make love in the dark
and mar the joys of Venus with blind motions?
The eyes are a lover's guide—
they show you what to do.
Seeing Helen naked
as she came from Menelaus' bed
was Paris' downfall they say;
naked too Endymion
won the love of Phoebus' sister
and held in his arms
                            the goddess naked.

So take your clothes off when you go to bed
or I'll tear them off; and then you'll know
what my hands feel like on your body;
and if my temper grows too hot
you'll have bruises to show your mother in the morning.
What have you got to hide?
Your breasts are firm;
for childbirth hasn't left its telltale mark on you.
So while the fates still grant us leave
let's feast our eyes on love
for the darkness of night is coming—
a long night with no day following.
As we cling to each other like this
bind us with a chain so strong
that time will not dissolve it.
Let's take as our pattern a pair of mating doves
(male and female in union complete)
If anyone seeks to set bounds to love's passion
he's a fool
for true love knows no limits.

And sooner will the earth
fool the farmer with unnatural fruits
the sun spur jet-black horses across the sky
the rivers call off their waters
and lead them back to the spring
and fishes lie parched and gasping
on a dry ocean bed
than I should look for someone else to suffer for.
Hers I shall be so long as I live—
and longer.
With nights like this a year would be a lifetime
and if she grants me many
(when a single night can make a god of you)
I'll live through all eternity.

If men could learn to take life lying down
drinking and making love
there'd be no butchering sword, no ship of war,
    and our bones would not be churned by the waters of Actium
nor Rome beleaguered
                                        by self-inflicted victories,
too tired to loose her hair in mourning.
Then our children's children would have something to praise us for
my cups are harmless and offend no gods.

While daylight lasts my darling
don't turn your back on the fruits of life.
For all the kisses you can give
                                                  will be too few.
Garlands wither and die
and the fallen petals float in the wine bowls.
Today we ride on the crest of love
but the end may come tomorrow.

16

Well, Cynthia, your praetor's back from Illyria
with profits for you
and suffering for me.
Had he left his life on some Ceraunian rock
what gifts I would give to Neptune.
But now there's feasting and drinking—and I'm not invited;
and the door stands open all night—but I'm not invited.

So do your job Cynthia:
there's fruit for the plucking
and a sheep for the fleecing
(one with more wool than wits)
and when you've taken all he's got and left him a pauper
tell him to go find
some other Illyria to sail to.
For Cynthia's not seduced by power and high office
the only thing that weighs with her
is the weight of a man's purse.

Help me Venus in my misery, grant me my prayer:
may he give himself a rupture
from too much sex.

Is love then for sale on the open market?
why for god's sake why
does she throw herself away on shoddy goods?
She tells me to dive in the ocean and fetch her some pearls
sends me to Tyre to look for souvenirs.
If only there were no rich men in Rome
and our leader himself

lived in a little hut with a thatched roof
then girls would have nothing to sell themselves for
they could grow old without moving house
and I wouldn't have to sleep alone for a week
while you soil your shining limbs
on that foul lout.

And it's nothing that I've done
(believe me Cynthia)
it's just that beauty (commonly speaking)
goes hand in hand with faithlessness.

This alien oaf comes strutting along in a state of erection
and suddenly there he is
reigning supreme in my kingdom.

How much do I have to take
before I learn to dry my tears?
or must this pain inevitably attend
on her misconduct?

The days pass by
and nothing interests me anymore,
a visit to the theatre,
a work-out on the Campus,
even my appetite is gone.
Shame on you, you say; yes, shame indeed.
But love, you know, is shameless
and doesn't listen.
Look at the great general who crammed the waters of Actium
with the empty hullabaloo of soldiers doomed to die;
at the promptings of his infamous love
he turned his ships about
and fled for refuge to the world's end.
(And this was Caesar's accomplishment
and Caesar's glory
that he used the hand that conquered
to sheathe the sword.)

I'd like to see all those presents he gave you
the dresses
the emeralds
the golden-gleaming topaz
snatched away by the gale
turned to dust and water in your hands.
Remember the necklace that brought no pleasure to Eriphyle
and the wedding dress that wrapped Creusa in flames of torment.
It isn't true
that Jupiter always smiles on the lies of lovers
and turns a deaf ear to their broken vows.
You've seen how the crash of thunder traverses the heavens
and lightning leaps down from its domain on high.
Don't say "it must be the Pleiads"
or "Orion's up—it looks like rain."
Thunderbolts don't fall for no reason.
That's Jupiter punishing girls for breaking their promises
(for he too has suffered at their hands).
I ask you is it worth it
to shiver with fear every time the storm winds blow
for the sake of a purple dress?

17

To say "come tonight"
and not to mean it
is to have blood on your hands.
This is the song I sing
for all those nights
that I have waited out the lonely hours
tossing all over an empty bed.
You can pity Tantalus
as the teasing waters leave him with parched lips
you can gasp at the labours of Sisyphus
as he rolls his troublesome load all the way up the mountain
but there is nothing in the world that lives more wretched
than a man in love
if you're not a fool be anything but this.
They used to call me happy
and look at me with envy
and now I have to work to gain admittance
once every ten days.
I'm even banned from sleeping on the streets
under the frosty moon
or smuggling messages in through a crack in the door.
O I could hurl my body from a flinty rock
or mix a dose of poison
and take it—in my hands.

And yet . . .
I'll never change her for another

and when she sees that I've been true to her
it'll be her turn to weep.

18a

It's endless quarrelling that leads to hate—
just keep your peace and she'll capitulate;
if you see anything say you didn't see it,
and if you feel it hurting—deny it.

*

Suppose that I were white with years
(just a hypothesis)
and my face was scored with wrinkles
and the skin hung loose:
When Tithonus was an old man
did Aurora love him less?

She didn't like to leave him
all alone at home;
as soon as she came back from work
she'd dandle him on her arm—
then she'd unyoke the horses
and give them a good groom.

And all night long she'd hold him
in her chamber in the East
complaining that the daybreak
must come again too fast.
She'd get onto her chariot
and call the gods unkind
then grudgingly go out to do
her duty for mankind.

O great was her lamenting
    when Memnon lost his life;
but her joys in old Tithonus
    were greater than her grief.

That girl was not ashamed to have
    an old man in her bed;
she didn't mind his kisses
    in spite of his hoary head.

So who do you think you are, you wretch
    to hate me when I'm young—
One day you'll be old and bent,
    and it won't be long.

*

But why should I care so much? that's just love's way:
yesterday's friend is his enemy today.

18b

So now you've started dyeing your hair—
have you gone mad?
parading in borrowed colours
like a Briton stained with woad;
if you look the way nature made you
you'll look the way you should.
What shame that a Roman head should glint
with French pomade.
If someone dyed her hair blue
(supposing that she could),
would it necessarily follow
that blue hair is good?
Girls who play tricks with hair dye
should suffer among the dead.

So wash it off; your beauty
will not be any less.
You're beautiful enough to me
if you keep on saying yes.

You have no son and no brother.
Why won't you be my ward?
And the bed we share together
can keep you under guard.
Then you won't have to sit around
elaborately coiffured.

Do nothing that would make me
believe what rumour says.
For the voice of reputation
leaps over lands and seas.

19

Although I didn't want you to leave Rome
without me Cynthia
I'm glad you're going to the country
far from the high road:
the air is clean there
there'll be no degenerate young man
to coax you into unchastity
no drunken brawling under your window
no voices shouting "Cynthia" to spoil your sleep.
You'll be all alone gazing on the lonely mountains
the flocks and fields
that make up the farmer's meagre estate
No games for your undoing
no temples—
your favourite place for sinning—
nothing to look at but the bulls plodding before the plough
and the vines being shorn of their leaves with skillful hook;
and you'll bring a tiny handful of incense
to a simple country shrine
where a kid straight from the fields
will crumple before the altar;
then you can tuck up your skirts and follow the steps of the dancers
safe from the eyes of uninvited males.

I think I'll go hunting;
I'm all agog for the rites of Diana
(Venus can take a rest).
This is the life for me—
tracking the wild game
hanging their horns as trophies on a tree
calling "Halloo!" to my eager hounds.

Not that I'd dare to flush out monstrous lions
or grapple hand to hand with wild boars
and yet I'm bold enough
to pounce on a timid hare as it lies in a trap
and bring down birds with a sticky rod
where the leafy banks of Clitumnus shade its lovely waters
washing the snow white oxen

And don't forget my darling
if your attentions wander
that I'll be coming soon
for the lonely woods
and the winding streams that flow from the mossy hills
can't stop me worrying
that somebody keeps on repeating your name.
When the lover's away
it's open season.

20

Why do you weep like Briseis
    or poor Andromache?
Why do you tire the gods with cries
    of my inconstancy?

More quietly mourns the bird of woe
    amidst the Attic leaves;
and Niobe's tears more gently flow
    down to her children's graves.

Though chains of brass should bind my hands
    and you were in Danae's tower,
for you my love I'd burst those bonds
    and leap that iron door.

My ears are deaf to what I hear,
    so why should *you* doubt *me*?
And by my parents' bones I swear
    (may they haunt me if I lie)
till darkness comes, my love, I'm yours:
    as one we'll live and die.

Suppose your fame and beauty
    should fail to keep me good,
I'd stay and do my duty
    in such gentle servitude.

Since first we set the town abuzz
    six times the moon's been full,
and often behind your yielding doors
    your bed has served me well;

you loved me then for what I was:
        such nights were not for sale.

Though you were always in demand
        you wanted me alone;
if I forget may I be damned
        before the judgment throne
with birds to peck my entrails and
        with Sisyphus's stone.

No need to write me suppliant notes;
        I'm still as true as ever.
For slow to stop and slow to start's
        my watchword as a lover.

21

For every lie
that Panthus told you in that letter
may Venus make Panthus pay.

But when it comes to the truth
wouldn't you say that I'm more accurate
than the oracle at Dodona?
He's got a wife
                    that gorgeous lover of yours.
Those wasted nights! Oh don't you feel a fool?
Look at him there he goes
singing as free as a bird
while you poor gullible you
                                        lie down alone.
They're talking about you now he and his cronies;
he's telling them with pride
of all the times that you were at home to him—
and he declined.
I'll bet my life you're nothing more to him
than a subject for boasting
a trophy to sustain him in his marriage.

It happened to Medea
thrown over by her erstwhile guest:
when Creusa came in
                              she went out.
And the Ithacan gave Calypso the slip:
the first she saw
                    he was spreading his sails to the wind.
Poor credulous girls
learn this lesson from your misfortunes:

think before you give.
But she (would you believe it?)
is looking around for someone else.
Didn't you learn *anything* the first time?

My love of course will go on
"any time, any place"
"in sickness and in health"
and so on.

22a

I don't need to tell you, Demophoon
of all the girls that charmed me yesterday,
and all the heartache that I suffered for it.
As I walk around the streets, every corner brings its reward.
And as for the theatre it was specially designed
for my destruction:
the snow white arms of the dancers swaying in sinuous motion,
the melodies on the lips of the singers;
and all the while my eyes range round the audience
looking for something to hurt them
the gleam of a naked breast
locks of hair that stray across a milky brow
pinned by a pearl at the crown.

You ask me why Demophoon
what is it that makes me soft on women;
love has no answer to the question why.
Why do people hack at their arms with ritual knives
slashing themselves to the crazy beat of the flute?
Nature gave every man a weakness at his birth:
it's my fate to be always in love.
Although I should suffer as Thamyras did for his singing,
I could never be blind to a beautiful girl.

If I look frail and skinny, it's not what you think.
For the cult of Venus involves no hard labour.
Ask around; there's many a girl can tell you
how I have manned my post the whole night through.
When Jupiter came to Alcmena he stopped the stars in their tracks
and two nights long the sky was without its ruler;
that didn't make him sluggish at his thunderbolts;

love never saps the strength you need for loving.
When Achilles went into battle straight from the arms of Briseis,
did the Trojans stand their ground before his spear?
And when ferocious Hector rose from the bed of Andromache,
do you think they didn't panic in the Greek ships?
Achilles was still a champion at knocking down walls,
Hector at burning ships—and I at making love.

The sky has two servants to light its lamp: the sun and the moon.
One girl is not enough for me.
If one won't let me in, I need another
to hold me and caress me with her loving arms.
And if she's in an angry mood and won't come,
I like her to know there's another who will.
It's safer to moor your boat with two hawsers;
and there's less to fear for a mother of twins.

22b

If you mean no, say no; if not, say yes.
What use in words if you don't say what you mean?
Nothing hurts a lover more than this:
to say you will, then suddenly decline.

With sighs and groans he tosses on his bed,
refusing to believe that she won't come,
tires out the slave with asking what she said,
and fears to find the answer still the same.

23

i

I used to shun the ignorant herd
and the crowded street;
but now I drink from the public springs—
and the water's sweet.

Does a freeborn man give bribes to another man's slave
when he wants to send a message to his love,
endlessly asking, "Where is my lady now?
Seeking the shelter of some shady porch?
Or promenading in the park?"
And when you've been through the labours that rumour ascribes to Hercules
you get her answer back: "What's in it for me?"
All for the privilege of seeing the sour face of the janitor
and having to closet yourself in his filthy quarters.
That's a high price to pay for one night a year—
I've had enough of girls who close their doors.

Give me a girl who throws back her cloak and walks like a free woman,
one with no guardians to fence her in with fear,
who wears out her dirty shoe-leather on the Sacred Way,
and when you ask her, doesn't keep you waiting.
She doesn't play hard to get, nagging and cajoling
till your skinflint father cries "Not another penny!"
Or burst out in a panic: "My god! Get up, please hurry.
Today's the day my husband's back in town."
Those are the girls for me—Syria's gift to Propertius;
in a "respectable" bed I feel like a burglar.

To be in love
is a state of slavery
for a man's a slave
when he's no longer free.

ii

"Keep away from love affairs!
you're hardly the one to talk:
Everyone knows about Cynthia
we've read the book."

That's enough to bring the sweat to anyone's temples.
A gentleman should learn to keep his love,
or keep his love life to himself.
But if Cynthia still breathed gently on me
they wouldn't call me the prince of debauchery
or drag my name through the city
in ridicule and contempt;
if I burned with lust, they wouldn't have to know.

That's why I keep to girls who walk the street:
they don't tell tales,
and that's worth a lot.

iii

She wants a fan of peacock feathers
some dice of ivory
a crystal ball to cool her hands,
trinkets that glitter on the stands
along the Sacred Way.
My god, I'd rather foot that bill
than be some cheating woman's fool.

24

Was it for this that you bid me be happy?
How can you be so lovely
and so false?
Just a night or two of love
and you call me a burden in your bed.
A moment ago you were praising me as you read my poems.
Is your love so quick on the wing?

Does he think he can match me for talent,
does he think he can match me for skill?
First let him learn to love in a single bed.
Would he go and fight with Hydras if you asked him to?
Would he bring you apples from the dragon's claws?
Would he swallow deadly poisons without a word?
Would he suffer shipwreck and swallow the salt water?
Would he put up with all this for you?
(Oh I'll perform your labours, try me my darling.)
Under that bluster you'll find he's a coward
puffed up by his bragging to inflated rank;
a year from now it'll be all over.
But nothing will make me change, not the Sibyl's long years
not the labours of Hercules, not the black day of death.

It's you who will gather my bones;
and you'll say as you put them to rest:
"Here lie the bones of Propertius, faithful to the last;
Oh, you were faithful indeed, though you had neither pride of birth,
nor riches to speak of."
There is nothing I cannot bear, no cruelty will change my heart:
your loveliness makes any burden light.
Certainly many have fallen for beauty like yours;

but it's certain that few have been true.
Theseus loved Ariadne
Demophoon loved Phyllis
loved them and went their way
breaking the laws of hospitality.
And you know the story of Medea and the Argo:
how she saved her lover's life—and he left her cold.

She's a hard woman who can offer her favours to more than one man,
and dupe them all with her counterfeit love.
Don't take me for one of your wealthy well-born lovers;
how many of them will still be there
as I will
to gather your bones on the last day?

Though I pray it may be you
who mourn for me
with streaming hair and naked breast.

25

No one but you so lovely
    was born to bring me pain:
So seldom fate allows me
    to hear you say "come in."

Your beauty in my verses
    all others will outlive,
(If Calvus grants me pardon
    and Catullus gives me leave).

The veteran lays down his arms
    and says good-bye to war;
and the aged ox will tell you
    that he pulls the plough no more.

Idle on the empty beach
    lies the rotting hull;
and the ancient shield, now out of work,
    hangs on the temple wall.

Though I lived as long as Tithonus,
    though Nestor were my name,
old age could never change me:
    I'd love you just the same.

*

Wouldn't it be easier
    to serve a tyrant cruel,
or groan with you, Perillus,
    in the belly of your bull?

Or look the Gorgon in the face
    and feel yourself grow hard,
or lie upon the Caucasus
    and let the vultures feed?

But though the iron sword blade
    is worn away by rust,
and drips can wear away a stone—
    yet I'll stand fast.

There is no threshold hard enough
    to wear a lover down:
for love is constant and endures
    the threats it didn't earn.

When met with scorn he asks for more;
    when wronged he takes the blame;
and though his feet should say him nay,
    he comes back all the same.

*

Don't put on airs my friend because
    your love is going strong;
remember that no woman
    can keep her word for long.

And when the storm's still blowing
    it's early to give thanks;
for the water in the harbour's full
    of floating spars and planks.

You don't demand your winnings
    when the race has just begun;
your wheels must graze the turning post
    seven times before you've won.

When love blows fair it plays you false
  and soon becomes a squall;
and the longer that you have to wait
  the heavier the fall.

Though she may love you, keep your joys
  locked silent in your breast:
somehow a lover's boastful words
  always come home to roost.

And though she asks you often
  remember to go but once:
for a love that makes men jealous
  is a love that has no chance.

If modern girls would still behave
  like ancient heroines,
then I would be where you are now:
  it's time, not you, that wins.

But I won't change my habits
  to suit the present needs:
for a man should choose his route himself
  and follow where it leads.

*

You say a man needs many loves
  if he's going to do his duty;
but think how our eyes would suffer
  from seeing so much beauty.

One girl is soft and lovely
  with delicate milk white skin,
another's a dusky beauty—
  how do you choose between?

You've seen the girls of Argos,
   you've seen the girls of Rome;
but when you watch them walking
   the effect is just the same.

One dresses in Plebeian cloth,
   one wears a scarlet cloak;
but when your heart is wounded
   there's no difference in the ache.

So if one girl is all you need
   to rob your eyes of sleep,
one girl's enough for any man—
   enough to make him weep.

26a

I saw you, darling, shipwrecked in my dream
plying with weary stroke the Ionian spray;
for every falsehood you confessed your sin,
and bowed your hair beneath the water's weight,
tossed like Helle on the livid deep
when she fell from the fleecy back of a golden sheep.

O how I feared some sea would bear your name,
and men would sail your waters in dismay.
I prayed to Neptune, Castor and his twin,
and you, Leucothoe, made divine of late.
Above the waves you stretched your fingertips,
and as you sank my name was on your lips.

If Glaucus had beheld those eyes of yours,
   then you'd be mistress of the Ionian sea,
and have to listen to the spiteful jeers
   of white Nesaee and blue Cymothoe.

But then I saw a dolphin swift to save,
   the one, no doubt, that bore Arion's lyre.
High on a rock I steeled myself to dive—
   and the dream faded, shattered by my fear.

26b

Now let the world exclaim
and glorify my name:
for I'm the king of love—
my mistress is my slave.

And not for streams of Lydian gold
or wealth of Persian kings long dead
would I be told
"Poet, leave my bed."

"I hate a wealthy lover"
she says, reciting me;
what girl was ever
a truer worshipper of poetry?

In love what counts the most
is faithfulness and trust;
when a man's a lavish giver
he's everybody's lover.

26c

My mistress plans to cross the seas.
Oh I'll come too: a single breeze
will waft two loving hearts.

One beach will be our sleeping place
one tree to shade us overhead
one spring for us to drink
and out at sea a single plank
on poop or prow's sufficient space
to be a lovers' bed.

And every risk I'll bear—
let savage Eurus lash
and chilly Auster drive
our sails to who knows where
come every blast
that tossed Ulysses on the deep
and wrecked a thousand Danaan ships
against the Euboean coast
come winds that made the twin rocks clash
when Argo's sailors sent a dove
to scout the unknown sea
let Jupiter's lightning flash
consume our ship with fire
if I am with my love
and my love with me.

Cast up on the shore
naked we'll lie together,
and if the earth shall be her grave
then wash me out to sea

and yet our love need have no fear
for Neptune's cruelty
for he's as versed in love
as Jupiter his brother.

Amymone should know:
when she went looking for a watering place
he ravished her in the field
and with his trident struck the earth.
Thus the god with his embrace
granted her vow
and water like a miracle poured forth
from an urn of gold.

Ask Orithyia about the North Wind:
the god that masters land and sea is not unkind.

Believe me, love, for us
Scylla shall grow less stern
and the whirlpool that with hideous jaws
sucks and spews in turn.
For us no stormy cloud
will veil the stars at night;
Orion and the Kid
will shine out clear and bright.

But if I have to die I'll die with pride
laying my life down at your side.

27

Death comes to mortals in his own good time;
why ask what hour or by what route he'll come?
Why scan the cloudless sky with Punic skill
to find the star that brings man good or ill?

Sailing to Britain, to Parthia by foot,
on either journey hidden danger lurks;
and we weep for fear of our lives when violence breaks
and the war god stirs the ranks to uncertain fight;
and houses can burn down, and houses collapse;
and the blackening draught should never touch your lips.

But the lover fears neither war nor the North Wind;
he knows when he must fall and by what wound.
Though he sit at his oar on Styx's reedy bed,
looking on the grim sails of Charon's bark,
let him catch but a breath of his mistress calling him back,
and he'll make the journey that the laws forbid.

28

i

Jupiter!
Pity my love in her sickness before it's too late;
  if you let such beauty die, yours is the crime.

Now is the season when the scorched air shimmers with heat;
  the Dog Star is up; and the earth is aflame.

But it's not the fault of the heat nor the crimes of heaven:
  think how often you've named the gods in vain.
That's what brings girls to grief and always has done:
  their oaths are snatched away by the wind and rain.
And it hurts Venus to hear herself compared:
  she's jealous of beauty greater than her own.
Have you been making mock of Juno's temples?
  Did you dare to say Athene's eyes were green?
Beautiful girls never know when they've said enough.
  It's your beauty and your tongue that brought this pain.

And yet this life of yours now wracked with danger
  will come more gentle at the end of day.
Io the goddess once lapped the Nile's waters
  and cowlike lowed her early years away.
Ino's wanderings are over; now frightened sailors
  call on her as divine Leucothoe.
And Perseus' famous wife Andromeda
  was offered once to the monsters of the sea.
At night men set their sails to Callisto's star,
  no longer a bear in the fields of Arcady.

And if the fates shall hasten your last sleep,
your fated tomb will bring you happiness.
You can talk to Semele; she'll understand:
she learnt like you that beauty's dangerous.
And all the heroines in Homer's epics
will stand aside and offer you first place.

Though fate has struck you down, you must bear its whims;
for god and destiny can grant reprieves.
Juno's a jealous wife, but she'll forgive you;
when a girl is dying, even Juno grieves.

ii

The bull-roarers are silent and the spells are all over;
ash from the bay leaves lies on the burnt-out hearth.
The moon is tired of climbing down from the sky;
and the black-winged bird is chanting its song of death.

If you have no pity for one, then pity us both;
for I'll be with her whether she live or die.
One trip from death's ferry with its dark sails spread
is enough to carry our love to the lakes of hell.

Grant my prayer and I'll pledge this song of thanksgiving:
"Great is Jupiter, who saved my darling's life."
And she'll be there, sitting in worship at your feet;
and as she sits she'll tell you
how death lingered close.

iii

Persephone stay merciful
Pluto be no more cruel.
Among the dead there are beauties in their thousands;

leave us just one for the world above.
Iope's yours,
and snow white Tyro's yours,
Europa
and the lustful Pasiphae—
they're yours,
and all the beauties of ancient Crete and Achaia,
of the ruined kingdoms of Thebes and the aged Priam.
Every Roman girl who made her mark
is dead and gone:
the greedy pyre has claimed them all.
Beauty is not forever,
and fortune doesn't last;
for every man his death is waiting
far off or near at hand.

iv

My love, my life, the danger's passed—
and you owe a dance to Diana,
ten nights of vigil to the heifer goddess,
and ten nights more for me!

29

i

Last night, my love, as I was wandering drunk,
no slaves to be my guide,
my path was blocked by a gang of tiny boys
(I couldn't count them—I was too afraid).
Some of them carried torches, some had arrows,
and some had fetters ready to put on;
they were all stripped for action; one of them, the ringleader
cried "Don't you recognise him? that's our man.
She gave us a job to do; now seize him quick."
With that a rope was tied around my neck.

One bid them shove me forward; another shouted
"He says that we're no gods—so let him die.
You fool to scour the town for common girls
while she waits for you hour by hour—I can't think why.
When she loosens the bands that tie her purple bonnet,
and her heavy-lidded eyes begin to move,
you breathe the scent of no Arabian herbs,
but a perfume made by love."

"Let him go, my brothers; he's promised to love her truly.
And look, we've brought him to the house she bid."
So they put their cloaks back on, and left me, saying:
"Now learn to spend your nights at home in bed."

ii

It was early morning; and I went to see
if Cynthia slept alone—alone she lay.

I stood there stunned: she'd never looked more lovely
    not even when she dressed in rich array
and went to ask advice from virgin Vesta
    in case her dreams were giving us a warning:
that's what she looked like lying there fresh from sleep;
    for beauty's power needs no adorning.

"What's this?" she said, "an early morning spy?
    do you think that I behave the way you do?
I only give myself to a single lover;
    and if you're not faithful, then it won't be you.
Show me the prints of a lover on my bed,
    show me the marks of our copulating limbs.
Come, can you smell that perfume on my body,
    the scent that gives away an adulterer's crimes?"

I tried to kiss her, but she pushed me away,
    jumped out of bed, and slipped her shoes on her feet.
So I'm the fool who spied on a faithful mistress.
    Since then I haven't spent a happy night.

30a

Where are you fleeing you fool?
there's no escape.
You can flee to the banks of the Don
but you won't outpace love.
Though you ride up aloft on Pegasus' back
give wings to your feet like Perseus
hurtle through the air with Mercury's sandals
slicing the breezes
you'll get no help from sky travel.
Love looms above you poised to swoop
love sits on your neck like a succubus
to break you in.
He guards his prisoners day and night
and keeps you with your eyes fixed on the ground.

But should you chance to stray
                    the gods will hear your prayers
if they come from a ready heart.

30b

Old men
with blunted sensitivities
can say what they like about your parties;
let us not waver, my love, from the path we have chosen.
For they can burden their ears
with the chanting of antique laws,
but this is the place for the cultured song of the flute.
(O flute unjustly thrown to drift on Maeander's stream
when it brought an ugly swelling to Athene's cheeks.)

So why should I want to sail over Trojan waters
and make for the shores of the Caspian sea
so the gods we share may be spattered with each other's blood
and a loathsome booty
brought to our ancestral shrines?

Is it any shame to me
that I live happy with a single sweetheart?
If you have charges to make, love is the offender.
Don't throw it in *my* teeth.

Come with me Cynthia
where the caves are moist with dew in the mossy hills,
and you'll see the Muses perched upon the rocks
singing of the secret love affairs
of antique Jove:
how Semele burned him up, and Io drove him mad
and he flew like a bird to the roofs of Troy.

No one has yet been able to withstand
the arrows of the winged god;

so why should I be put in the dock
for everybody's crime?

And don't be afraid that you'll bring a blush
to the modest cheeks of the maidens
for they too know what loving is—
if it's true what they say that a certain person
lay pressed beneath Oeagrus's handsome body
on Thracian rocks.

Let them set you in the forefront of the dance
with Bacchus in the middle
carrying the wand of poetry
and then I can bear the sacred ivy
hanging in clusters on my brow:
for without you
                    I have no power of song.

31

You ask me why I'm late?
Phoebus' golden portico
has just been opened by the mighty Caesar.
What a sight it was
its Punic columns planted in rows
and in between them the daughters of old Danaus—the whole gang.
And then I saw Phoebus
looking more lovely than the god himself
his marble lips opened to sing
to his silent lyre.
Around the altar stood a group of cattle,
four oxen made by Myron's hand
that seemed to breathe with life.

And there in the middle bright with marble the temple rose
(even Delos where he was born
is not more dear to Phoebus);
over its pediment the chariot of the sun;
and its doors a splendid work of Libyan ivory—
one showing the Gauls as the rocks of Parnassus sent them flying,
the other mourning for Niobe's dead children.

Inside between his mother and his sister
the god himself
the Pythian
sings in his trailing robes.

32

To see you is to seduce you;
not to see you is not to desire you:
thus the fault is in the eyes of the beholder.

But why are you forever trying your luck
at Praeneste's oracle
and visiting the battlements that Telegonus built?
What's your chariot doing on the road to Tivoli
and the ancient Appian Way?

Here is the place for your promenading Cynthia
when you have time to kill.

What worries me is all those people
who watch you running to the grove to worship
with your torches burning
carrying fire to the goddess of the crossroads.

Pompey's colonnade I know
is far too squalid
with its shady columns
and its famous awnings stiff with gold,
its avenue lined with towering plane trees,
the waters cascading from the sleeping Maron,
the nymphs around the basin lightly prattling,
and the Triton that suddenly spouts.

Don't be a fool—your journey tells your secret.
It's not the city you're avoiding
but my sight.

You're wasting your time spreading nets for me—
I'm wise to all your tricks.
But it's you not me who'll suffer
when you get the name you deserve
for I've been hearing rumours about you that sting my ears
ugly rumours—and the city's full of them.

But you don't have to listen to their spiteful tongues
gossip like that has always been
the penalty for being beautiful.
It's not as though they called you a poisoner
(Phoebus above will testify your hands are clean)
and if you've spent a night or two
playing the endless games of love
why should I be disturbed
by peccadilloes?

Tyndaris left her home for an alien love
but they passed no sentence
and she came back alive,
And Venus herself, so the story goes, succumbed to the lust of Mars;
Yet she kept her place of honour among the gods.
Ida can tell you how Paris the shepherd was loved by a goddess
and they lay together among the flocks
watched over by the tree nymphs, her sisters,
and a band of old-timers
with father Silenus at their head—
your companions, Oenone, when you went apple-picking
beneath the caves of Ida
catching the fruit as it fell in the palm of your hand.

When whores are swarming like bees
there's not much point in cross-examination
to find out how a girl got rich.
For Rome today is blessed beyond belief
if a single girl steps out of line.
Why, Lesbia's done it all before;

and what's the harm in following precedent?
Anyone looking for stern old Sabines like Tatius
hasn't been long in our city.
For sooner could you drain the ocean dry
or pluck the stars from heaven with your mortal hand
than keep our women chaste:
that fashion's been out since Saturn's day.
At the time when the waters of Deucalion flowed over the earth
and in these post-diluvian days
can you tell me of any mortal
who kept her bed intact
or any goddess
who lived content with a single god?
They say the wife of mighty Minos fell
for a raging bull as white as snow;
and Danae though walled with brass
hadn't the strength to say no to Jupiter.

So take as your example
the heroines of Greece and Rome.
Live free
for I acquit you.

33

i

Now once again begins the gloomy rite:
    ten nights of worship Cynthia must fulfil.
I curse this festival that Io brought
    to Roman matrons from the tepid Nile—
for one who keeps a lover from his mate
    is a cruel goddess, call her what you will.

When you and Jupiter had your affair
    you must have learnt what it's like when the going's hard:
for Juno gave you a pair of horns to wear;
    and when you opened your mouth to speak you mooed;
you cropped the oak leaves and made your lips all sore,
    and back from pasture just sat and chewed.

But now he's given you back your human face
    what an imperious goddess you've become!
Won't Egypt's dark-skinned votaries suffice?
    Why did you ever take the road to Rome?
What do you gain if women sleep without men?
Take my advice and grow your horns again.

If not I swear we'll drive you from our city;
    the Nile will always be the Tiber's foe.

*

But when it's over and I've earned your pity
    let's make the journey three times in a row.

ii

Your ears are deaf and all my words escape;
now Icarus' team plods slowly past the turn;
Why can't you put your dice away and sleep?
it's the middle of the night—but you drink on.
I curse the man who first discovered grapes
and stained the water's innocence with wine.

When Icarus was slain by the peasant's wrath
he learnt that wine's bouquet has a bitter sting;
and wine it was that caused Eurytion's death,
and the Cyclops found the Ismarian brew too strong:
wine spoils your beauty and destroys your youth,
and wine makes girls forget where they belong.

O God, she's lovely even in her cups—
drink on: for wine can't hurt your loveliness.
When round your bowl the wilting garland droops,
and you read my poems in that husky voice,
pour out Falernian till the tables swim
and the golden goblet's foaming to the brim!

When a man's away the tide of love will swell;
but constant access wears your value out.

Yet no girl sleeps alone of her own free will:
there's one thing love won't let you do without.

34

i

Don't trust the god of love with a pretty girl:
    that's how I almost lost my sweetheart.
Mark my words, there's no such thing as a friend in love:
    if she's beautiful, it's each man for himself.
That god's a defiler of kinsmen, a wrecker of friendships,
    and calls a man to arms against his comrade.
As a guest beneath his roof the adulterer came to Menelaus,
    and Medea left home to follow a stranger.

So Lynceus my false friend you dared to make a pass;
when you lifted your hand
didn't it fall back limp?
It's lucky she stood firm and never faltered.
Could you have lived with that crime on your conscience?
You can plunge your sword in my heart, or dose me with poison,
but keep your hands off my girl.
You can share with me body and soul
be lord and master of all my property
but not my bed, please keep away from my bed:
even Jupiter isn't welcome there.
Why I'm jealous of my own shadow—
a neurotic fool who fears when there's nothing to fear.

I'm letting you off this time—for one good reason:
you'd drunk too much and your words were wandering.
But you won't take me in again
with your furrowed brow and your ascetic ways—
even a philosopher knows
that love is part of "the good life."

ii

So my old friend Lynceus is madly in love at last.
A special welcome to our latest convert.
And you might as well forget
that wisdom you culled from Socratic books
those lectures you give on "the movements of natural bodies."
The book Aratus stayed awake to write
can't help you now;
your antique friend has nothing to say about love.
You'll find Philetas makes a better model
or the dream of slender Callimachus.

So sing if you must those well-worn themes:
—Achelous
and how love broke his flow
—Maeander
winding over the Trojan plain like a maze
playing catch-as-catch-can with its own waters
—Adrastus and his talking horse
that sulked at Archemorus' funeral
when he won the race
—the chariot of Amphiaraus engulfed by fate
and the downfall of Capaneus sweet to Jupiter
But it won't do a bit of good:
stop building buskinned verses like a second Aeschylus
and loosen your limbs to a gentler measure.
Now is the time to pare down your poems on a narrow lathe
and let the fires that burn in your heart
soften your tough verses.
Or else you'll fare no better
than Homer or Antimachus:
those mighty gods mean nothing
to a beautiful girl.

But a bull won't yield to the heavy plough
till you've locked his horns in the noose.

No more could you unaided
bear the harsh travails of love:
you're still wild and I'll have to break you in.
Girls don't want to know the answers to these questions:

    what makes the world go round?
    why does the moon grow weak before her brother's horses?
    what's left of us beyond the Stygian waters?
    is there any meaning in the thunderbolt?

Just look at me
no family fortune came my way
no triumphant grandfathers
from wars of long ago
but here I am king of the banquet with girls all around me
—and it's all thanks to that talent which you scorn.

iii

So leave me to loll at my ease amidst last night's garlands
touched to the marrow by the shaft of the unerring god;
while Vergil sings
of Actium's shore where Phoebus keeps watch,
and Caesar's stout-hearted fleet.
And now he's rousing Aeneas to arms
and building city walls on the Lavinian shore;
Stand back, make way, you poets of Greece and Rome—
something is coming to birth, something greater than the Iliad.

And you sing as well of Daphnis and Thyrsis
wearing away their pipes with playing
beneath the pines that shade Galaesus' stream;
or how to seduce a girl with ten apples
and a kid from its mother's teats.
How lucky you are

    to get your loving at bargain prices!
    Why even Tityrus could afford to sing
    and be refused;

and lucky Corydon
          seeking to pluck the fruits of virgin Alexis
          the farmer's sweetheart.
And though he's resting now tired out with his piping
his praises still are sung
by the good-natured wood nymphs.
And you sing the precepts
of the ancient poet of Ascra—
what's the best soil for corn to thrive in
what's the right slope for a vine.

Such are the songs you sing to your well-tuned lyre
as though Apollo himself
were running his fingers over the strings.

iv

But the reader will find something to please him
in poetry like mine
whether he's a novice in love or an old hand.
For the sweet-voiced swan, though not so loud of mouth,
outsings the untutored goose.
Here Varro sported
                    once Jason's journey was over
ablaze with love for his Leucadia.
And this was the song Catullus sang
in frisky verses
that made the name of Lesbia more famous than Helen's.
This was the theme laid bare on Calvus' well-wrought pages
as he sang of poor Quintilia's death.
And Gallus when he died
still smarting from Lycoris' beauty
bathed his wounds in the waters of the underworld.
So Cynthia will live in the lines of Propertius
if fame will let me join that company.

BOOK THREE

1

Callimachus, Philetas,
your venerable ghosts I beg and sacred rites
to grant me entrance to your grove.
For I am the first to come
consecrated by the clear spring water
bearing in my hands the mysteries of Italy
as I dance the dances of Greece.
Tell me what cave it was
where together you shaped your slender song;
and how did you enter? with what foot?
and drank what water?

Don't waste Apollo's time by keeping him under arms;
let your verse go slim and pumiced fine.
That's what lifts me in fame to the skies
while the muse that I begot is borne in triumph,
her horses crowned with wreaths;
and beside me in my chariot sit tiny cupids
and poets swarm behind my wheels.
Why gallop headlong struggling for the lead?
the muse travels a narrow road
and there's no room to pass.

There's many will add
new chapters of glory to your annals Rome
singing the day when Bactra marks the bounds of empire.
My page has brought the songs of peace
down from the muses' hill
by a route no man has trod.
Maidens of Hippocrene tender be the garlands
you offer to your poet;
a tough and spiny crown won't suit my brow.

And what the envious mob withholds while I'm still living
fame will repay with interest when I'm dead.
For death and the passage of time make all things grow;
when your last rites are paid
your name comes greater to the lips of men.
For who would know of the towers that fell to a wooden horse
of rivers grappling with a Thessalian hero
Simois flowing from Ida, Scamander child of Jove,
and the wheels that three times fouled the corpse of Hector
dragging him over the plain?
Why even their native soil would barely remember
Deiphobus and Helenus and Polydamas
and the military exploits of Paris (such as they were)?
There'd be no talk of Ilion
of Troy twice captured by the power of the god
who burned on Oeta.
Yet the mighty Homer who chronicled their fall
has known his work grow great with time.
And so shall Rome praise me
through generations yet unborn.
I, who will then be ashes, prophesy that day.
My bones will lie in no forgotten tomb,
with just a stone to mark the place,
if Lycian Apollo hear my prayer.

2

Now let my song resume its normal round
so girls may thrill once more to the well-known sound.

They say Orpheus' lyre could charm wild beasts
   and stop raging torrents in their courses;
they say music built the walls of Thebes
   moving stones from Cithaeron to take their places;
and Galatea hearing the Cyclops sing
   grew calmer and turned back her dripping horses;
no wonder then that Bacchus and Apollo win
   hordes of girls to pay homage to my verses.

Though I can't boast a mansion built on marble pillars,
   ivory ceilings fretted with golden beams,
apple trees to rival Phaeacian orchards,
   fancy grottoes watered by Marcian streams,
I have songs to charm my reader, and the muses
   dance to my measure with untiring limbs.
You're a lucky girl, if this book sings your praises:
   your beauty lives forever in my poems.

Wealth that aimed pyramids at the stars,
   the temple at Elis, Jupiter's earthly home,
the splendid sepulchre of Mausolus—
   all these are subject to death's final term;
fire and flood will steal away their pride,
   or the years will bring them crumbling to their doom.
But a poet's skill can never be destroyed:
   his name stands deathless till the end of time.

3

I dreamed I was lying in Helicon's tender shade
beside the spring that flowed
from Bellerophontic hoof;
Alba your kings and kings' exploits
I strained my mouth to sing
putting my tiny lips to that full-flowing stream
where Father Ennius once quenched his thirst;
and in my dream I sang
    —of Curii and Horatii their pikes and pillars
    —of the royal trophies that Aemilius carried
      in shipboard parade
    —of Fabius' triumphant waiting game
      of ill-starred Cannae and the gods
      who turned to hear our prayers
      and the Lares pitching Hannibal from the hearth of Rome
    —of Jupiter saved by the voice of the goose. . . .

But Phoebus spotted me from the Castalian grove
and spoke to me like this
standing by a cave resting his arm on his golden lyre:
"You fool, such mighty streams are not for you.
Who bid you set your hand to epic labours?
Not there your hope of fame, Propertius;
drive your frail chariot where the grass is soft.
So girls who wait alone to meet a lover
may pick your slender volume from the footstool
then toss it down and pick it up again.
Your verse has gone careering off the track—
and the little boat that bears your genius
will sink beneath the weight.

One oar should strike the waters while the other
grazes the sand—for that's where safety lies.
It's out at sea that the going's rough."

He spoke, and with his ivory plectrum
motioned me to a seat
along a path new-cut from the mossy earth.
There was a grotto here
verdant
set with a mosaic of tiny stones
and from its pitted dome of rock
hung tambourines
the mystic objects of the Muses cult
and Father Silenus modelled in clay
and the reeds of Arcadian Pan.
And the birds of Lady Venus
my mates the doves
were dipping their crimson beaks in the waters of the lake
Gorgonean.
And the nine maidens, each to her allotted task,
fashioned their gifts with tender hands:
one gathered ivy for the thyrsus, while another
tuned her voice to the lyre string, and a third
kept both hands busy weaving a garland of roses.

And one of them, a goddess among goddesses,
(from her looks I'd say Calliope)
took me by the hand and said:
"Travel on snow white swans, and you'll be content;
and never let the snorting warhorse
lead you into battle.
It's not for you
to sound the call to arms on the strident bugle
or ring the Aonian grove with war;
or to tell of the fields of battle
where Rome stood firm beneath the Marian standard
and smashed the Teutons' power;

or how the barbarian Rhine
flowed with the blood of the Suebi
as it bore their mangled bodies on its sorrowing waters.
You'll play another fanfare—
of garlanded lovers on thresholds not their own
and the drunken brawling of a midnight rout;
and teach the spells that charm girls from behind locked doors
(or how to score a hit on a surly husband)."

So spoke Calliope
and drawing from the spring where once Philetas drank
she touched the water to my lips.

4

War the god Caesar plots for the wealthy Ind;
his ships will plough the waters rich in pearl;
fit gain for heroes—triumph at the world's end,
Tigris and Euphrates flowing beneath your rule.
At last she'll feel the rods of Italy,
and Latium will be home to Parthian booty.
You ships well-tried in war, put out to sea;
go forth in arms, you horses, do your duty.
I sing good luck: wipe out the Crassi's shame,
and write another chapter to our fame.

By father Mars and Vesta's fateful fire
I pray that I may see before I die
the wheels of Caesar heaped with the spoils of war
and hear the cheers that make the horses shy;
I'll lie in my sweetheart's arms watching the sights:
the pictures of captured cities with their names,
the arrows of trousered horsemen swift in flight,
the captive chieftains pinned beneath their arms.
Venus protect your child till the end of time
so the name of Aeneas may live on in him.

Let those who earned it bear the spoil away,
and leave me to stand and cheer on the Sacred Way.

Love is the god of peace;
it's peace we lovers worship.
For though I fight pitched battles with my mistress,
no lust for gold gnaws at my heart:
I need no jewelled cup to quench my thirst,
no thousand acre farm to plough
of fat Campanian land;
and plot no senseless rape of Corinthian bronzes.

It was a poor job that Prometheus did
moulding the primal clay—
he botched man's heart;
his skilful design of the body ignored the mind:
he should have got the mind right first.
So now the storm winds toss us out to sea
as we go looking for enemies to fight
and weave an endless chain of war.

You fool
you'll take no riches with you to the shores of Acheron:
naked you'll travel on the infernal ferry.
For victor and vanquished are mingled in death:
Marius and Jugurtha sit side by side
the consul and the captive;
and Croesus of Lydia stands not apart
from the Ithacan beggar.
That death is best that comes when fate decrees it.

My pleasure is
to dwell while I'm young on Helicon's slopes
linking hands in the Muses' dance;

and to wreathe my mind with the chains of the loosening god
and my brow with spring roses.
And when the oppressive years leave Venus stranded
and old age flecks my black hair white
then it shall be my study
to understand the ways of nature:
what god it is who orders with his skill
this cosmic household;
what causes the moon to rise and fall,
and every month return
its crescent horns bent round full circle;
where are the winds from, lashing the salt spray,
the tug of the gusting Easterly,
and the clouds that never run dry;
and whether the day will come when the world's battlements crumble;
why does the rainbow drink the rain;
why do the peaks of Pindus tremble;
why is the light of the grieving sun
borne on shrouded horses;
why does Bootes drive his cart so slowly,
and the Pleiads dance in a fiery cluster,
what stops the ocean flowing beyond its bounds,
why does the year complete its cycle
in four seasons;
and are there gods below to judge us
giants in torment
rabid Tisiphone shaking her venomous locks
Alcmaeon with his Furies, and the starving Phineus,
the wheel
the rocks
the throat that's parched amidst the waters
and Cerberus with threefold maw
guarding the cave of Hell
and Tityus confined
to a mere nine acres;
or is it all an empty story
passed down the generations

of pitiable mortals,
and there's nothing to fear beyond the grave.

That's what I look for as my life's end.
But you whose pleasure lies in making war
go, bring back home the Crassan standards.

Lygdamus, if you want your freedom
tell me the truth about our mistress.
Don't swell me up with imagined joys,
making up stories to meet my desires.
A messenger's job is to stick to the facts,
and a slave who lies is risking his neck.
Tell me the truth then, right from the start,
all you remember—my ears are thirsty.

You saw her like that? her hair in a mess?
the tears streaming from her lovely eyes?
No mirror lying on the bed?
No jewels decking her snow white hands?
her arms draped in a dress of mourning?
her makeup lying on the floor forgotten?
the house gloomy, and the maids all glum
carding their wool while she sat and spun,
snatched up the yarn to dry her tears
telling of our quarrel in a breaking voice:
"Lygdamus, tell me, is that what he promised?
an oath's an oath, though a slave's my witness.
Could he throw me over without any reason
and set up house with—that kind of woman?
Is he glad that I'm pining in bed alone?
let him leap for joy when I'm in my tomb.
These are the charms she used to match me:
spells and brews and a wheel to witch him,
poison from a swollen toad,
bones of a snake sucked dry of blood,
feathers of a screech owl found in the grave,
fillets of wool from a dead man's bier.

But the time will come, if my dreams aren't liars,
when he'll kneel at my feet and pay full price;
and his bed will be empty for spiders to weave in;
and Venus will sleep when they do their loving."

If that's what she said, and she really meant it,
back where you came from, Lygdamus, quickly,
give her this message, and say I was weeping;
my love can be angry, but can't deceive her;
like her I suffer in flames of torment—
twelve days now, and I swear I've been faithful.
And if peace comes from such a conflict,
then, Lygdamus, you'll get your freedom.

7 

So it's money, money that fills our life with care
and makes us tread death's route before our time;
it offers a cruel diet to feed man's vices,
and from its stem sprout troubles like vine-shoots.
That's what made Paetus spread sails for Egypt,
then tumbled him time and again in the frantic waters:
the search for money cost him his young life.
And somewhere his body is floating
an exotic meal for distant fishes;
and never can his mother pay her dues
to the gentle earth
and lay him to rest amidst the family tombs.
His bones are the haunt of seabirds
and the vast expanses of the Carpathian Sea
serve as his burial mound.
O fell North Wind
who held Orithyia scared in your clutches
was there such booty in it for you?
And Neptune why should you exult
in that shattered hull?
they were guiltless men who sailed in her.
Paetus why tell of your youth?
why call your mother's name with drowning lips?
the sea has no gods to listen.

You were moored for the night on the rocks,
and the storm winds rose
wore through your cable and ripped away your hawsers.
A tomb stands on that shore
remembering Agamemnon sick at heart,
marking the spot where Argynnus made amends

to the menacing waters
(in grief Atrides kept the fleet at Aulis
and paid for that delay
with the slaughter of Iphigenia).
Give back the body of Paetus to the dry land
(for his life rests in the waves)
let the sand come and cover him:
there's sand enough to spare.
So the sailor passing by
may look on the tomb of Paetus
and tremble though his heart be brave.

Go on, then, build your curving ships;
fashion your instruments of death.
Man has invented a new way of dying
with his own hands.
The land alone was not enough
so we added the waters to the territory of fate
skilfully multiplying the routes to disaster.
If your household gods can't hold you back, what chance has an anchor?
and what does a man deserve
if his land is not enough?

All your dealings lie in the wind's power;
no ship has ever died of old age;
and the harbour itself is a treacherous haven.
For nature spread the waters smooth to catch man's greed.
One prosperous trip is more than you can hope for.
The conquering fleet was smashed on the rocks of Caphareus
and the wreckage of Greece was strewn over the salt waste.
And one by one Ulysses wept for the loss of his comrades:
for he couldn't play tricks on the sea.
Had he taken my advice
content to plough his fields with the family ox,
he'd have lived in sweet companionship
before his household gods
a poor man—but a poor man on the land
wouldn't have needed to weep.

And how could Paetus bear the storm winds whining
and the rough ropes tearing his delicate hands?
He was used to a chamber of citrus and terebinth
where he pillowed his head on feathers like the rainbow.
The waves had ripped his nails from the living flesh,
and he gulped the loathsome sea water
clinging to a tiny plank
while the cruel night looked on.
So many evils joined forces
that Paetus should die.
Yet he sobbed one final prayer, one last lament
as the inky waters choked his dying lips:
"Gods of the Aegean, lords of the waters, winds,
waves that break heavy on my head,
where are you carrying me
plundering my life's first bloom?
With slender hands I ventured on your waters.
And now I'm to be dashed against the jagged rocks
where only the halcyons live.
For Neptune has raised his trident and aimed it at me.
I ask only this:
that the tide may cast my body on Italy's shores;
it is enough that what's left of me
rest in my mother's arms."
Then the eddying waters sucked him down,
and his life ended with these words on his lips.
O hundredfold daughters of Nereus, maidens of the sea,
and you, Thetis,
(for you have felt a mother's grief)
you should have held his sinking head above the waters—
he wouldn't have weighed heavy on your arms.

Be sure of this, you pitiless North Wind,
never will you look on my sails.
Far from the busy world I'll end my days
laid up on my mistress' threshold.

8a

I loved that quarrel yesterday in the lamplight,
  I loved the wild and bitter things you said,
when fighting drunk you shoved aside the table
  and threw the brimming wine cup at my head.

Come scratch my cheeks with elegant fingernail,
  grab at my hair in handfuls, do your worst,
take up the torch and threaten to burn my eyes out,
  tear off my tunic, strip me to the waist.

If you weren't in love, you wouldn't get so angry:
  for anger is a symptom of love's heat.
The girl who spits out insults in a frenzy
  grovels as helplessly at Venus' feet

as one who rings her lover round with spies,
  or rushes like a maenad through the city,
sees nightmares every time she shuts her eyes,
  shudders at portraits if the girl is pretty;

for I have learnt to read with soothsayer's art
the signs of true love in a victim's heart.

God keep my friends from women that are meek:
  for true love never comes without a fight.
Let people see her teeth-marks on my neck;
  my bruises tell them where she spent the night.

I long to moan in love or hear you moaning,
  to weep myself, or see you shedding tears,
when you fix me with a scowl that's full of meaning
  your fingers tracing words that no one hears.

I dread to sleep in peace and never sigh;
Love keep me pale and keep her temper high.

When Paris shared the joys of love with Helen,
  the clash of warfare added to her charms;
while Greeks advanced, and Hector stood to face them,
  he fought his greatest battles in her arms.

I'm going to fight you now and never cease,
or fight to keep you—anything but peace.

8b 

Go on, rejoice; you've earned your pride;
  if I could find a girl as fair,
    I'd teach you to regret.

May you who snared her in your net
  be pestered by a Father-in-Law
    while Mother waits inside.

That night she gave you in her bed
  it wasn't for your benefit,
    but mine, to fix the score.

9

i

Maecenas
knight from the blood of kings
Etruscan born
it's your ambition
to keep to the near side of your destiny;
so why send me
to travel a trackless sea of writing?
my tiny craft's not built for billowing sails.
I'd be ashamed
to lift a load I could not carry
and buckle and fall beneath the weight.

For different subjects fit different talents
and there are crowns to win
from more than a single peak.
This was Lysippus' glory:
                                        his statues breathing life
the boast of Calamis:
                                        his horses perfectly wrought
Apelles' masterpiece:
                                        a picture of Venus
Parrhasius' claim to fame:
                                        the art of the miniature
the tableaux of Mentor add a story line to beauty
while round the cups of Mys
the acanthus winds its narrow path
for Phidias Jove cloaks himself in ivory
and the fame of Praxiteles
is safe in the stone of his native city.

One man with his chariot
   makes victory keep pace
another with his speed of foot
   is born to win the race
one's a soldier trained to fight
   another lives in peace
Each follows where his nature leads
   for nature sows the seeds

ii

On you, Maecenas, I pattern my life
and have to answer you
by quoting your example.
The lordly axes of Roman government
are yours for the asking
you could set up your edicts in the market place
you could march against the warring Medes
till the arms hang thick upon your walls;
yours is the power from Caesar, and the wealth
that flows unceasing to your purse.
Yet you hold back
and huddle low in the insubstantial shadows
furling the sails that belly in the wind.
And mark my words the wisdom of your choice
will bring you like a second Camillus
onto the lips of men;
you'll stand at Caesar's side in the hall of fame:
for this shall be Maecenas' true memorial—
he was a faithful friend.

I'm not the one to spread my sails
and scud through the heavy swell.
I'm more at home in the shelter of a tiny stream.
I shall not weep for Cadmus' citadel
sinking into paternal ashes,
or the battles that ended in a fatal draw;

I shall not sing of the Scaean Gate
of the towers of Troy that Apollo built
and the ships of the Greeks
that came home ten springs later
when the wooden horse by Pallas' art victorious
broke up the walls of Neptune
beneath the Danaan plough.
I'll be content if my poems bring delight
in Callimachus' company,
and I sing the tunes Philetas sang,
so boys may burn and girls may burn to read them,
cry out my name and worship me as a god.

iii

Show me the way and I'll sing you an epic
of Jupiter under arms
defending heaven against the Titan thrust
struggling with giants on Phlegra's heights;
I'll tell of Roman bulls
cropping the lofty Palatine,
of city walls
built to last on the blood of Remus,
of twin kings suckled by a beast of the forest.
Lead on: my powers will grow to your command.
I'll follow the chariots as they ride in triumph
from furthest shore to furthest shore;
I'll tell how Parthians with bows unstrung
play no more tricks of flight,
Pelusium's barricades were cracked by the Roman sword,
and Antony served as his own executioner.

So cheer me on
holding gently the reins of my youth
signalling "go" to my hurtling chariot.
For this is the glory you grant me
and its yours to grant
that I followed in the footsteps of Maecenas.

10

I wondered why the muses
were standing by my bed
so early in the morning
as the sun shone red.

Today's my sweetheart's birthday:
they came to give the sign,
then clapped three times to bless her—
now let the day begin.

Give us a cloudless sky today
and calm the raging winds,
and may the pounding breakers
lap gently on the sands.

This day may I not look
on any grief or woe;
even on Niobe's rock
may the tears no longer flow.

And may the halcyons cease
their plaintive song and rest,
and the mother hush her bitter cries
for Itys lost.

And you my darling—you were born
under a luck star—
get up and greet the listening gods
and say your birthday prayer.

Then splash cold water in your face
   to drive away the sleep,
and set your shining hair to rights
   with skilful fingertips.

And do you remember the dress you wore
   a long time ago
when first you caught Propertius' eye
   and wouldn't let him go?
Well, put it on; and don't forget
   the flowers to wreath your brow.

Your strength is in your beauty;
   pray it may last for ever:
then you'll be mistress in your realm,
   and I shall be your lover.

Hang garlands on the altars,
   perform the sacred rite
and let the flare of incense
   fill the house with light.

And then it's time for feasting;
   let's drink the night away;
uncork the jar of saffron,
   breathe in the sweet bouquet.

Dance, for the night is young,
   till the flute can play no more;
and tell me each erotic thought
   you dared not tell before.

What's the point of sleeping,
   when the company's so good;
on with the party, raise a din
   to fill the neighbourhood.

Let's play at fortune telling,
  let's throw the dice and see
whether the wings of Cupid beat
  harder on you or me.

And after many cups of wine
  when the moment's right
and Venus has prepared us
  to consecrate the night

let's perform the ritual
  the birthday gods demand
lying in bed together—
  where birthdays ought to end.

11

Why should it surprise you that she twists me round her finger,
  and drags me where she wants to, a slave to her command?
Why do you accuse me of trying to malinger,
  when her yoke is on my shoulder, and I cannot burst the bond?
Wouldn't you ask the sailor if the storm is growing stronger?
  Couldn't the soldier tell you why he fears the wound?
You might have heard me boasting like you when I was younger.
  Look at me now and tremble: perhaps you'll understand.

Remember Medea
driving fiery bulls beneath a yoke of adamant,
sowing the seed of battle that made the soil bear arms,
clamping shut the fearsome jaws of the guardian serpent,
to bring the golden fleece to Thessaly.
And Penthesilea
ferocious on horseback
daring to draw her bow on the Danaan ships,
and when the golden helmet fell from her brow
vanquishing her victor with her loveliness.
Remember Omphale
who bathed in the waters of the Lydian lake;
the fame of her beauty reached so far
that the hero who tamed the world
and set up his pillars to prove it
turned his rough hand to the carding of wool.
And Persian Semiramis
built the great wall of Babylon,
layer upon layer of close-packed brick:
two chariots could meet on it and pass
without so much as a scrape;

she led the Euphrates in triumph
through the city she had founded,
and Bactra bowed its head to her command.
Enough;
why pick on heroes and single out gods for blame
when Jupiter has put them all to shame?

And what about that woman
who brought our weapons into disrepute
(she was good for a quick rub in the servant's quarters),
demanding as the price for her foul liaison
the walls of Rome and the senators her slaves.
Alexandria baneful city
treachery's best breeding ground
Memphis too often bloody to our cost
where Pompey's three triumphs
were wiped out in the sand—
(and Rome will bear that scar forever.
Better that you had died on Phlegra's plain
or bowed your head to Caesar)
And so that whore
queen of Canopus city of vice
the one and only scar we bear
from Philip's blood
presumed to set her baying god on Jupiter,
subject the Tiber to the Nile's abuse,
silence the Roman trumpet with rattling castanets,
chase Liburnian battleships with barge poles,
spread out her filthy canopies on the Tarpeian rock,
and sit in judgment
amidst the busts and arms of Marius.
What was the good of breaking the axes
of Tarquin proud in word and deed
to be ruled by such a woman?
Sing out your triumph Rome
and pray long life to Augustus
who kept you free.

She fled to the wandering waters of the frightened Nile
and held out her hands to the fetters of Romulus.
On her arms I saw
the fang marks of the sacred serpents
as the deadly paralysis crept through her limbs
and I called to Rome in a voice that was thick with wine
"Is that what you were frightened of
with such a citizen to defend you?"
The city that stands aloft on seven hills
watching over the world below
thrown into panic by the weapons of a woman!
These walls were built by gods
and there are gods to guard them.
Rome while Caesar lives
need have no fear of Jupiter himself.
Have you forgotten the ships of Scipio,
the standards of Camillus,
the Bosporus conquered by Pompey's hand,
the spoils of Hannibal, the monuments
to Syphax beaten,
the pride of Pyrrhus shattered at our feet.
Curtius built his monument
when he plugged the gaping earth;
Decius spurred his horse
and burst the enemy ranks;
there's a street that tells how Cocles stood alone
as they broke down the bridge behind him;
and the raven gave Corvinus
his name to keep.
And Apollo will tell the story of Actium's rout
when a single day
wiped out that mighty war machine.
Remember sailor
as you sail the Ionian Sea
whether you're heading for home or you've just left harbour
remember Caesar.

12

Postumus left his love and went
to fight in Caesar's regiment.
Did Parthia's spoils attract you so
when Galla begged you not to go?
A plague on all greedy men
who leave their beds to fight for gain.

Now while your greatcoat wraps you up,
and you use your helmet as a cup,
she pales and thinks each rumour true—
your courage will be the death of you,
and give some Persian bow delight,
some armoured steed and ironclad knight;
and they'll bring your remnants in an urn—
for that's how fighting men return.

Postumus lucky in your love,
far luckier than you deserve;
she has no fear to fence her in,
and Rome's the capital of sin.
Don't worry: Galla's not for sale,
she'll soon forget that you were cruel,
and when fate sends you safely back,
throw faithful arms around your neck.

You'll be a second Ulysses,
unharmed by all those long delays:
ten years of fighting, Ismarus' sack,
    the Cyclops with his eye burned out,
the clinging Lotus, Circe's trick,
    Scylla, Charybdis' waterspout.

The oxen Phoebus' daughter fed
 were roasted bellowing on the spits;
he left the nymph to weep in bed,
 was cast away for days and nights,
He saw the spirits' dark abode,
 his oars were deaf when the Sirens sang,
he revived his bow with the suitors' blood,
 and ended all his wandering,

and found his faithful wife at home.

And Galla's the Penelope of Rome.

13

You ask why girls have set their price so high
that a night of love can lead to bankruptcy.
Isn't the reason obvious at a glance?
We set no limits to extravagance.
Ants send us gold that's mined in Indian hills,
The Red Sea gives us Aphrodite's shells,
from Cadmus' city comes the purple dye,
and cinnamon from perfumed Araby:
such weapons can storm any virtuous door,
and make Penelope resist no more.
Whole fortunes deck the matrons who parade
flaunting the profits of their shameless trade.
He's quick to ask, she's eager to bestow;
if she delays, the offer is too low.

In Eastern countries which the dawn paints red
there's a splendid custom when the husband's dead:
his faithful band of wives stand round him vying
to be allowed the privilege of dying,
eager to share with him the final flame,
to burn in triumph, not to live in shame,
offer their bodies to the blazing pyre
and kiss their husband's lips with lips of fire.
Our Roman matrons are a faithless breed:
Evadne's gone, Penelope is dead.

Happy the peaceful country lad of old,
whose wealth was in his crops, not in his gold.
He gave his sweetheart quinces from the trees
and punnets heaped with crimson raspberries,
plucked violets and piled the baskets high

with lilies white to match her purity,
and brought her grapes still dressed in living green,
and little birds with plumes of changing sheen.
These are the gifts these rustic lovers gave
for secret kisses in a woodland cave.
Their only blanket was a roebuck's skin,
and the soft grass made their bed for loving in;
they lay within the pine tree's gentle shade
and watched the goddess naked—unafraid.
The ram could lead the sheep back home again,
their bellies full, to the unguarded pen.
And every god that watches fields and herds
blessed their dwelling place with kindly words:

"Welcome to my hunting grounds.
I've hares in plenty for your hounds
and birds to catch with fowler's rod:
for I am Pan, the huntsman's god."

The groves are empty and the shrines brought low;
for gold's the only god men worship now.
Faith is in exile, laws are bought and sold,
conscience that needs no law gives way to gold.
The doors of Delphi's shrine are scorched and black
where Brennus paid for his impious attack;
and mount Parnassus shook its laurelled brow
and crushed the Gauls with an avalanche of snow.
Gold was the reason Polymestor pressed
a hideous welcome on his Trojan guest.
His horses vanished, Amphiaraus gone
so his wife could put a golden bracelet on.
Proud Rome can't bear the weight of her own success;
Listen my country, remember the prophetess
who spoke the truth but no one heard; recall
no one believed that Troy was going to fall.
Paris, she said, will seal his country's fate;
beware the horse that's slithering through the gate.
That tongue that could have served her country well
must learn to bear the truths her gods foretell.

14

I much admire the Spartan wrestling schools,
but most of all I like the women's rules:
for girls and men can wrestle in the nude
(the Spartans think such exercise is good);
naked they throw the ball too fast to catch,
and steer the creaking hoop in the bowling match,
stand waiting, grimed with dust, for the starting gun,
and bear the brunt of the Pancration,
put boxing gloves on hands so soft and fair,
and whirl the heavy discus through the air,
gallop the circuit, helmets on their brow,
buckling a sword to thighs as white as snow;
with hoar-frost on their hair, they join the chase
as the hounds of Sparta climb Taygetus,
like Amazons, breasts naked to the fray,
who bathed in Pontic streams at the end of day,
like Helen training on Eurotas' sands
with nipples bare and weapons in her hands,
while boxer, horseman, champions to be,
her brothers watched, and did not blush to see.
In Spartan custom lovers may embrace
without concealment in a public place.
Girls aren't afraid, or locked up under guard;
no stern-faced husband makes the going hard;
you need no go-between to pave the way:
speak for yourself, and suffer no delay;
they wear no purple robes to cheat and lure,
no perfumed hair with overworked coiffure.
In Rome your little finger is too large
to make its way through a woman's entourage.
The lover can't get close enough to find

the proper way to ask—he's working blind.
If Roman girls would do as the Spartans do,
then, Rome, I'd have more cause for loving you.

15 

So help me, as I tell you true,
no more rows: one night's enough
to lie awake and think of you.

When I took my baby toga off
and used my newfound liberty
exploring on the paths of love

Lycinna first instructed me
to temper passion with finesse
(and oh! she gave those lessons free);

but three years now (or not much less)
and half a dozen words have been
our only form of intercourse;

my love for her is dead and gone.
Since then no other girl but you
has held me with her gentle chain.

So help me, love, I tell you true.

Here's a story about a girl who couldn't forget the past:
   queen Dirce thought Antiope had slept with Lycus
so she vented her spite on her, tearing out her lovely hair,
   sinking her ruthless nails in those tender cheeks;
she piled her with hanks of wool, far more than the other girls;
   and gave her a squalid hovel for her lodgings,
where she'd nothing to rest her head on but the hard ground,
   and even a drop of water was too much to ask.

Jupiter, did you see her suffering, her hands chafed raw
by the cruel shackles, and didn't come to the rescue?
Are you a god? and aren't you ashamed to see her a slave,
Antiope, your love? who else should she call on?
Yet all on her own, straining her body's strength to the limit,
she burst the royal fetters on her hands,
and ran away on frightened feet to the heights of Cithaeron.
Nighttime; the ground patched with frost; nowhere to rest;
so she blundered on, starting at the sound of the running river,
thinking it was her mistress on her trail,
till she came to a hut, her own sons' hut, but they turned her away
(Zethus unbudging, Amphion touched by her tears).
Like the waves of the sea coming to rest after a great storm,
when the winds have ceased their head-on clashing,
and the waters lap gently along the quiet beaches,
she sank to the ground, falling on her knees.
At the last moment they recognised her—she was saved by the bond of love.
Old man, fit guardian for the children of Jove,
you gave the sons back their mother—and the sons took Dirce
and lashed her to a raging bull to be dragged to her death.
This is Jupiter's doing, Antiope; to your great glory,
Dirce is carried to her many resting places
and the fields of Zethus are spattered with blood, and up on the mountain
the rocks ring with Amphion's victory song.

Don't try to make Lycinna smart;
you've seen what jealousy can do,
and it's hard to stop it once you start.

And anyway it isn't true;
don't listen to the tales you hear
it's you I'll love, and only you

when I am ashes on a pyre.

16

Midnight—and her orders came:
"To Tibur. I'm waiting. Come quick!"
(Ah! Tibur, the twin spires that gleam,
the tumbling falls, the spreading lake.)
Am I to trust the shrouded night,
hands in the darkness raised to kill,
or put it off till morning's light,
and face a weapon sharper still.
Those gentle hands can treat me rough:
one year in exile was enough.

Yet though on Scythian shores I rove,
or stroll on Sciron's rocky route,
No one will harm a man in love,
no one's as barbarous as that.
With moon and stars acting as guide,
and love keeping my torch alight,
the mad dog turns his jaws aside,
and I go safe by day or night.
I haven't got the blood to spill;
and Venus walks beside me still.

And if they killed me, what would I care?
I'd pay the price to die for love.
She'd scatter garlands on my pyre,
and sit and watch beside my grave.
Don't bury me in public ground,
where folks will come and laugh at me,
but in some small forgotten mound,
or underneath a shady tree
far from the tramp of vulgar feet:
I want no name-plate on the street.

17 

Bacchus YOU
yours is the altar I crouch at now
breathe gentle father
gentle on my sails
you with the power to still
love's frantic gusting
with wine the painkiller
coupler disuniter YOU
sluice this folly from my soul
this thing (you know what I mean
Ariadne on lynx-back
has written your record in the stars)
stoking the fires in my bones
has two antidotes
death
        & wine
night alone undrunk
racks a man tosses his heart
hoping and fearing all over the bed
soak my blazing temples with your benison
serving a summons on sleep
to enter my bones
and vines I'll plant you
                    whole rows of them
                    terraced hills of them
                    (up all night keeping off predators)
till the must is thick on the vats
and my feet stained purple

To you Bacchus horns and all
I dedicate my life

hailed laureate of your exploits
I'll sing
your premature delivery by thunderbolt
maenads routing the armies of India
the self-defeating frenzy of Lycurgus
against the newfangled vine
the body of Pentheus ripped
in triple tug of war
Tuscan sailors leaping
                    sinuous
      dolphin-bodied
out of the vine-filled ship
your streams flowing fragrant
          ("why Naxians are wine drinkers")
                              through the heart of Naxos
translucent your shoulders
                      draped
                              with thick hanging ivy
Bassarid hair encircled
                      with Lydian turban
sweet scented
                  on smooth-skinned neck
                                        the oil flowing
barefoot with trailing robes
                                beating the rhythm
Theban girls drumming
                            the suggestive beat of the tympanum
reed pipes opening their mouths to sing
                                          to goatfoot Pans
and right next door
                the great goddess Cybele
                with crenellated diadem
pounds the clanging cymbal in the dances of Ida
Before the temple doors
the bowl the priest the golden ladle
pouring the sacrament of
wine
YOU

all this I'll sing to you
high on my buskin
taking deep breaths
booming like a Pindar
disencumber me
of this arrogant servitude
bow down my troubled head
with sleep.

18

Shades of Avernus shelter the sea at play;
on Baiae's tepid pools the steam hangs low;
they buried Misenus here in the sand, Troy's bugler,
and the traffic rumbles over Herculean causeway;
here too stretching out his hand to the cities of men
came the god of Thebes to the clash of cymbals.
But what god now, accursed murderous Baiae,
squats malignant in your waters?
Down he was dragged into Stygian deeps,
and on your pools still drifts that mighty spirit.

Nobility, virtue, a mother's devotion,
the house of Caesar in his arms,
the canopies fluttering over the crowded theatre
(his mother had seen that everything was just so)
counted for nothing: in his twentieth year his life stopped short;
time crammed it all into that narrow span.
Go on, then, think big, dream of triumphs,
of standing ovations in the theatre,
of cloth of gold and jewel-encrusted Games—
so many free gifts to the funeral pyre.

But we're all headed that way, highest and lowest alike,
everyone must tramp that uncongenial path,
wheedle their way past the three-throated cur,
and climb aboard the general ferry with its grim-faced old-timer.
Go, build yourself a shelter, wall yourself with brass and iron,
and death will drag you out head first.
Nireus' beauty didn't save him, nor the strength of Achilles,
nor Croesus' wealth, spawned by the streams of Pactolus;
and the ordinary soldier was cut down in droves by the plague,

paying the price for Agamemnon's second love.

No passenger for you here, ferryman of the shades:
the soul is gone from the corpse they are carrying,
gone where Caesar went and Claudius, victor of Sicily—
he has left the paths of men and reached the stars.

19

Don't preach me sermons with the same old text:
that men in general are oversexed.
Remove the bridle, take away the bit,
and women just can't get enough of it.
The blazing fields of corn may quench their flame,
rivers may turn and flow back whence they came,
Syrtes may offer peaceful anchorage,
Malea a haven when the storm winds rage,
but nobody can hold a woman back
when passion sends her racing round the track.
Pasiphae loved a bull and met disdain,
so she dressed up as a cow and tried again.
And Tyro, whom the river set alight,
in Neptune's streams went down without a fight.
Myrrha burned for her aged father's bed,
and sprouting leaves concealed her as she fled.
Medea too (or should I save my breath?)
appeased her passion with her children's death.
When folk called Pelops' house the house of whores
why add that Clytemnestra was the cause?
And Oh! that treacherous dowry Scylla paid;
the gates stand open wide, the town betrayed;
she sold her father to be Minos' wife,
cut off his hair, his kingdom and his life.
Oh! brighter burns your torches, maids unwed—
he dragged her from the stern till she was dead.
And that's why Minos sits as judge below:
though victor, he gave justice to his foe.

20a

Do you think he still remembers what you look like,
that one who hoisted sail and left your bed?
What kind of man would trade his love for profit?
All Africa's not worth the tears you shed.
So leave the gods alone, your words are empty:
he's found some other girl to hug instead.

You're beautiful, and skilful as Minerva;
a famous poet makes your lineage bright;
and all that's missing is a faithful lover—
I'm faithful, darling: come to me tonight.

20b

Hurry up, Phoebus, chivvy the sun
  dawdling across the summer sky.
And if there's dawdling to be done
  I pray the moon may linger nigh
and watch us celebrate the rites
  of love new-born. O night of nights!

Before we finalise the deal
  we'll draft a contract, clause by clause,
all guaranteed by love (his seal),
  witness: the goddess crowned with stars.
We'll talk for hours, discussing terms,
before love gives the call to arms.

No contract—and you'll lie alone
  without a god to bring redress;
the bonds of lust are soon undone;
oh, may these vows that make us one
  ensure our faithfulness.

Let him who violates the god
  that seals a lover's sacred pact,
let him who in another's bed
  pollutes the holy nuptial act
feel all the pains that love can bring
be lashed by scandal's prating tongue
weep for his mistress all night long
  and find her windows locked
always in love without love's usufruct.

21

A good long trip, that's what I need,
to Athens the city of culture;
perhaps travelling will help me to forget.
Seeing her just makes the pain grow worse
love feeding on itself.
And every other escape route
is blocked by the god's presence.
Not tonight, she says, and not tonight,
and when she gives a grudging yes,
she sleeps on the edge of the bed
all wrapped up.
Travel's the only way: leave Cynthia well behind—
and out of sight will be out of mind.

Come, my comrades, put out to sea,
draw lots for rowing stations,
run the sail up the mast;
the wind blows fair, not a cloud in the sky.
Rome's skyline fades; farewell. Farewell, my friends,
and you, my sometime sweetheart, fare you well.
First time afloat as a guest of the Adriatic
I'll make my prayers to the boisterous gods of the sea;
with the Ionian behind us
the yacht resting its weary sails
in Lechaeum's calm waters
I'll slog it by foot across the Isthmus
that fends off sea from sea.
Back on land in Piraeus' harbour
then up the long arms
to the city of Theseus.
And there I'll put my mind in training

in Plato's gym
or the gardens of Epicurus
(doctor of philosophy)
or study the art of Demosthenes (armed to the teeth)
or the salty volumes of Menander
(doctor of wit) . . .
or anyway I'll put my eyes in thrall
to the paintings
the ivories
the bronzes
worked by the hands of masters.

Time and distance
will heal the wounds in my silent heart.
And if I die, I'll die when fate decrees it,
not crushed and broken by a worthless love;
and death will come without shame.

22

How can you stand it, Tullus, all these years
in frigid Cyzicus
where the waters of the Propontis wash the isthmus,
where Cybele stands on Dindymus
fashioned from a vine-stalk,
where Dis the rapist drove his horses?
amidst the delights of the cities of Helle,
think how I miss you, Tullus.

You can do your sightseeing
where Atlas carries the sky on his shoulders
and Perseus chopped off the Gorgon's head;
go look at Geryon's cowsheds,
at the prints that Hercules and Antaeus made
wrestling in the dust,
at the dancing places of the Hesperides;
or take a boat and row yourself to Colchis
retracing the route of the Pelian bark
as it sailed through the clashing rocks
coached by Argo's dove,
that pine tree pressed into shape as the world's first prow;
Ortygia's worth seeing, they say, on the banks of Caystros,
and the river that guides its waters in seven streams;

but all the wonders of the world
are not a patch on Rome;
nature has lavished all its blessings here:
a soil where warriors thrive and violence fails—
Proud stands your story, Rome, in the records of fame:
strong in the sword, in justice and compassion
supreme, we hold our wrathful hand in victory—

the Anio at Tivoli, the Clitumnus
rising among the wooded hills of Umbria,
the Marcian aqueduct built to eternity,
the lakes of Alba and the Grove
that share a common stream,
the clear spring of Juturna
where Pollux watered his horses.
No horned snakes here slithering on scaly bellies,
no waters seething with nameless monsters,
no clanking of chains
as Andromeda pays for a mother's crime.
In Italy we serve no banquets
for Phoebus to shudder at and turn his back.
It wasn't here that mother plotted against son
and burned up his life in absentia;
that Pentheus was treed by a pack of frenzied maenads,
and a smuggled deer
cast off the Danaan fleet.
It wasn't here that Juno bowed the horns
for her husband's mistress
misshaping her beauty as a common cow.
No Sinis here to crucify you on pine trees,
no Sciron with his unfriendly rocks,
no beds to cut you down to size.

This is the land that bore you, Tullus,
this is your lovely home.
Here there are honours to be won that match your birth;
Here there are citizens worthy of your eloquence,
a prospect rich in grandchildren,
and a wife to match your love.

23

My writing tablets lost, those literate slabs,
all those words of wit and wisdom gone!
Time had worn them smooth, where my finger rubs,
so they bore my seal without my signet on.
They had a language of their own, they could pacify
sulky girls without a word from me.

Their value didn't lie in plates of gold:
they were made of dirty wax and cheap boxwood.
But they kept faith and did as they were told:
what more can you ask, if the results are good?
They carried secret messages, e.g.:
"Where were you yesterday? What took you so long?
Have you found another girl, prettier than me?
Or do you imagine I've done something wrong?"
Or maybe: "Come today; we'll be alone.
All night long we shall be Cupid's lodgers."
(You know how clever girls can prattle on
fixing the hour for love's sweet subterfuges.)

But now some miser, counting up his hoard,
writes down his horrid sums and keeps his tabs.
O give them back—I'll offer a reward:
A PURSE OF GOLD FOR A PAIR OF WOODEN SLABS.
Go find some pillar, boy, and post this bill—
and add that your master lives on the Esquiline hill.

24

You're not half so lovely, woman, as you think.
That beauty existed only in my eyes.
It was love produced those praises, Cynthia,
love made me stupid enough
to glorify you in my verses
dressing you up in elaborate figures
to make you seem what you were not,
comparing your cosmetic glow
to the rosy dawn.

No family friend could steer me clear,
no witches wash me clean in the vast sea,
surgery, cautery, shipwreck
couldn't force the truth from me.
I was trussed hand and foot
roasting in Venus' oven.

Dry land at last.
Look at the garlands on my prow:
The Syrtes are behind me, and my anchor's dropped.
I was tossed and battered in the monstrous surge—
now consciousness returns.
My wounds have closed.
If there's a goddess of sanity
I dedicate myself to her
for all my prayers to Jupiter
fell on deaf ears.

25

I was the latest after-dinner joke.
Everybody had their Propertius story.

Old faithful, with five years of service.
Now bite your nails and think what you've lost.

No weeping—I've been had that way before.
Tears are Cynthia's secret weapon.

I'm weeping too, but what hurts more than leaving
is having a mate who pulls against the harness.

Farewell threshold, thanks for your sympathy.
Good-bye front door; I never quite knocked you down.

But as for you, may you be hunted by the silent years,
your face ravaged by the ugly burden of time

frantically plucking the white hairs from your head
facing your wrinkles in the accusing glass

your turn to find out what rejection feels like
an old hag reaping what you've sown

Learn to read in my prophetic page
the terrible outcome of your beauty.

BOOK FOUR

1

i

Look around you, stranger;
all you can see, the grandeur of Rome,
was grass and hills before Aeneas came.
Up there on the Palatine
where stands the monument to Phoebus the sailor
the cows of Evander huddled like refugees;
from gods of clay those golden temples grew,
and a simple shack was a respectable dwelling.
There was nothing but bare rock
for Tarpeian Jove to thunder from;
nothing but cows
to greet the Tiber passing by.
There's Remus' house rising above a great flight of stairs:
there was a time
when a single fireside was a whole kingdom.
The Curia shines proudly now
with purple-togaed senators,
where once sat peasant Fathers dressed in skins,
in the days when the sound of the horn summoned the folk to assembly,
and a meadow was good enough for the Hundred to meet in.
No hollow theatres draped
with rippling awnings,
no stages to exude the scent
of festive saffron.
And why should one search for gods to import
when the people trembled on tenterhooks
before the ancestral rites?
—the yearly bonfire of straw at the Parilia,
docking the tail of the October Horse (just like today),

donkeys hung with garlands as a treat
to penurious Vesta,
cheap victims in procession
headed by scrawny bulls,
stuffed pigs touring the tiny precincts,
the shepherd offering up his sheepguts
to the sound of the pipe,
the skinclad ploughman plying his bristling whip
(and hence our Lupercal
when anything goes).

No hostile weapons gleamed on those rude warriors:
they fought with charred stakes—nothing else.
Lycmon set up his headquarters
wearing a cap of skin,
and the power of Tatius was in his sheep.
Such were the Titii, the Ramnes, the Luceres,
such were the men that Romulus led
driving his four white horses,
in the days when suburban Bovillae was bigger than Rome,
when tiny Gabii was a vast concourse,
Alba a great power
(the sign of the white sow come true)
and Fidenae a sabbath day's journey.
For the breed of Rome
had nothing to inherit but a name
proud fosterling of a she-wolf.

You did well, Troy, to send us your exiled gods;
that Dardan ship was borne on favouring wings,
kept safe from harm (for signs were good from the start)
when the belly of the horse debouched its contents,
when son carried father perched trembling on his neck,
and the flame forbore to burn those dutiful shoulders.
That's where the courage of Decius came from, and the axes of Brutus;
and Venus in person brought Caesar his arms,
the conquering arms of resurgent Troy.

Blessed the land that received your gods, Iulus:
for the quaking Sibyl on her tripod at Avernus
proclaimed that Remus of the Aventine
should sanctify this soil;
and the words came true at last
that the Trojan prophetess sang to aged Priam:

"O Greeks turn back your horse,
your victory is vain;
for Jove will arm this dust and ash,
and Troy will rise again."

She-wolf of Mars, best nurse of our fortunes,
what a city you have suckled.

That city now I seek to reconstruct
in reverent verses; I haven't got the lungs
for thundering, but this tiny trickle of song
such as it is I offer
to the service of my country.
Let Ennius wreath his verse with shaggy garlands;
stretch forth to me your leaves of ivy, Bacchus—
and my volumes will make Umbria swell with pride,
Umbria, the birthplace of Rome's Callimachus;
and people will look on those hilltop towns
that clamber out of the valleys
and honour them because of me.
Rome bless this work that rises in your name,
bright be your omens citizens, and may the birds
sing me good luck,
while I tell of Troy's downfall and Rome from Troy reborn,
of years of danger over land and sea,
of rites and festal days and ancient place-names:
that is the goal my sweating horse must strain for.

ii

"Where are you off to, Propertius, rushing madly into prophecy?
That's not the way the fates have spun your thread.

These songs spell trouble: Apollo will turn his back
as you force the words from your reluctant lyre.

For I am HOROS
the prophet who's never wrong
(or call me a beginner
who never turned a sphere);
credentials unimpeachable
begotten of Babylonian Orops
(scion of Archytas)
third generation from the house of Conon.
I've lived up to my lineage, as god's my witness;
in my predictions truth comes first.
Gods have become good business nowadays:
falsifying Jupiter for profit,
or the yearly markings of the sun's ecliptic,
or Jove the bringer of blessings, or violent Mars,
or Saturn that weighs heavy on us all,
the meaning of Pisces and Leo the brave,
why Capricorn bathes in the western sea.

When Arria was for sending her twins to war,
fitting on the armour though the gods said no,
I told her straight: 'Thy sons will ne'er again
bring home those weapons to the family gods.'
There are two graves now to show that I was right.
Lupercus on horseback was shielding his wounded face
when his horse stumbled and caught him unawares;
while Gallus on guard duty, looking after the standards,
fell dead before his eagle's bloody beak.
Poor boys, twin victims of a mother's greed.
I wish my prophecy had not come true.
Again when Cinara had been long in labour
and the weight within her womb was slow to budge,
'Offer to Juno' I said 'and thy prayer is granted.'
She gave birth—and my prophecy triumphed again.

That beats Jove's sandy cave in Libya,

or the entrails that articulate
the god who is lodged within,
the augur interpreting the flight of crows,
or necromancers looking for ghosts in bowls of water.
If you want the truth, study the highway of heaven,
the infallible path of the Zodiac
and the fivefold zones.
Calchas is a grim warning; it was he who launched
the ships that clung to the holy rocks of Aulis;
he dipped his sword in the throat
of Agamemnon's daughter,
and the father hoisted bloodstained sails.
But the Danaans never came back; O Troy despoiled
fight back your tears and look on the coast of Euboea;
under the cover of night
Nauplius planted the avenging fires
and Greece became a floating corpse
drowned by the weight of her booty.
Ajax conquering hero
choose out your candidate for rape
wrench the prophetess from the protecting robe
against Minerva's interdict.

So much for stories.
Now to the business of your horoscope;
compose yourself to weep afresh.
Ancient Umbria bore you, and your gods are famous
(well, am I right? did I get it in one?)
where the dew falls on Mevania's misty plain,
the Umbrian lake grows warm with summer waters,
the peak of clambering Assisi
is crowned by a wall
a wall made famous by your genius.
You gathered the bones of your father before your time;
you were forced to live in poverty
though you'd plenty of bullocks to plough your fields
till your farm was lost to the grim surveyor's rod.
When you took the golden amulet from your callow neck,

and put on the toga of freedom
watched by your mother's gods,
Apollo quoted a few lines from his repertoire,
and banned you from thundering in the frantic forum:
'Go fashion elegies, a crafty job;
provide a model for the scribbling mob.
March out to war with Venus' armour on;
and give some target practice to her son.'
Now all those triumphs that you toiled to win
are brought to mockery by a single girl.
You can wriggle off the hook, but what's the use?
her gaff will get you by the snout.
It's she who tells you whether it's night or day;
your teardrops fall at her command.
No point in barring the door or posting a thousand sentries:
if she makes up her mind to deceive you
she'll crawl through a crack.

Fear not when your ship is labouring in the storm,
or you march unarmed against the foe,
or the hollows quake and the earth gapes wide,
but BEWARE THE SIGN OF THE CRAB."

2

You think I'm good at metamorphoses?
Well, let me introduce myself:
I am the god Vertumnus;
place of birth: Etruria
nationality of parents: Etruscan
  —though I must say I never regretted
    leaving Volsinii when the war was on.
    I like the people here;
    and what do I want with an ivory temple?
    all I ask is a view of the Forum.
The origin of my name: well, long ago
the Tiber journeyed where I'm standing now;
they say you could hear the sound of the oars on the water.
But he gave it as a present to his foster children—
and hence the theory that Vertumnus means
"the stream that turned" [Lat. Versus Amnis].
Another theory: the first fruits of the year
are offered to me as season follows season
[Lat. Vertens Annus].
                                        The first belong to me
when the grapes change colour on the purpling bunches
or the long-haired wheat grows fat with milky grain.
You can see the cherries at my feet, the autumn plums,
the mulberries ripening on a summer day;
and the grafter brings his offering of thanksgiving—
a garland of fruit with apples grown
on a grudging pear tree.

It's a slanderous lie, that's not what it means at all.
it's my name, so I ought to know.
And anyway I'm a god.

I've a natural talent as an impersonator:
you choose the part, I'll play it to perfection.
Dress me in silk, I'm a maiden soft and winsome;
give me a toga, my manhood speaks for itself.
With a scythe in my hand and a crown of plaited straw,
you'll swear I've just done mowing the grass.
I've been a soldier under arms, got mentioned in despatches;
I've been a reaper, bowed beneath my basket.
In court I'm sober as a judge;
but put a garland on me and you'll shout aloud:
"the wine has gone to his head."
Wrap me in a turban and I'll masquerade as Bacchus;
a plectrum's all I need to do Apollo.
In a helmet I'm a hunter; with a pole in my hand
I'm the patron god of bird catchers.
Then there's Vertumnus the charioteer
or the stuntman leaping from horse to horse;
a fisherman in a broad-brimmed hat, a travelling salesman
all spivved up in a trailing tunic;
or a shepherd hunched to his crook, or a nurseryman
trudging along the dusty road with his baskets of roses.
—that's one thing about me that goes without saying:
people offer to me the pick of their gardens.
My trademark is the dark-green cucumber,
the pot-belly gourd, the cabbage
with its wrapping of slender rushes.
And every flower that opens its mouth in the meadow
looks lovely wilting on my brow.
So Latin gave me a name to suit my behaviour:
Vertumnus the omnivert.
As for the rest that's Rome's present to the Tuscans
(that's why they call it Tuscany Row)
for the time when the people of Lycmon fought as comrades
and smashed the arms of Tatius, the wild Sabine.
I saw it all myself—the battle line faltering,
the weapons dropping from their hands,
the ignominious flight.

But grant me this, god-begetter,
that togaed Romans till the end of time
may bustle at my feet.

Just a few lines left; you there
rushing to meet your deadline at the courts,
I won't keep you long; I'm on the home straight.

I started life as a maple stump
hacked into shape by an impatient pick axe
a poor god in a friendly city
in ante-Numa days.
But Mamurius caster of bronze—
may the Oscan earth not chafe those craftsman's hands—
had the skill to mould me into pliant service
one statue—with a hundred claims to fame.

A letter from Arethusa
to her dearest Lycotas:
(mine, did I say, when I never see you?)
If there's anything you can't read,
the blots and smudges are made by my tears,
and where the letters are indistinct,
those are the marks of a dying hand.
So Bactra gets to see you—
yet another Eastern tour—and the armies of China
mounted on iron clad chargers; the wintry Getae,
Britain in chariots and paint, the swarthy Indian
pounded by the waters of the rising sun.
Is this the meaning of our marriage vows?
are these the nights you pledged me
when I yielded up my arms?
(I was just a beginner and you drove me hard.)
The torch that led me home was lit
from the sombre flames of a ransacked funeral pyre;
I was sprinkled with the waters of death, and on my head
the chaplet sat askew: the marriage god
did not attend my wedding. All those gates
hung with my offerings—that did more harm than good:
I'm on my fourth greatcoat now.
Curse the man who plucked
the first stockade from an undeserving tree,
and fabricated the insistent trumpet
from blaring bones.
He's a better candidate than Ocnus
for sitting sideways twisting rope
feeding his hungry donkey to eternity.
Your corselet, tell me,

does it blister your delicate shoulders?
does the heavy javelin chafe those hands
not made for fighting?
I'd rather that than have to weep
for someone else's love bites on your neck.
They say you're looking pale and thin; I trust
you got your pallor pining for me.
As evening turns to bitter night
I kiss your weapons (those you left behind)
complaining that the bedclothes won't lie still,
begging the birds to sing
and make the morning come.
I work through the long winter nights
spinning a soldier's wardrobe—cloaks
from best quality Tyrian fleeces—
and studying military objectives:
the course of the river Araxes,
questions of logistics:
how long can the Parthian cavalry go without water.
I take a map and learn the painted world by heart;
I know how god the craftsman laid it out,
what lands are numbed with cold
or decomposing in the heat,
and what's the wind that bears a ship to Italy.

Only my sister keeps me company,
and my nurse grown pale with my heartache,
swearing (forswearing) that there's nothing to worry about:
it's just a "routine seasonal delay."
Lucky Hippolyte, lucky barbarian,
a warrior with naked breasts,
a helmet on her lovely head.
So why can't Roman girls go on campaign?
Oh take me as part of your marching gear,
and I'd follow you (no straggling) over Scythian mountains,
where father Jove with an icy grip
binds fast the waters.
For great is the power of love, but greater still,

when man and wife are together,
and Venus is there in person
fanning the flames.
And what do I want with dresses of shimmering purple,
and rings on my fingers of translucent crystal?

It's all so quiet
dead silence in the house;
every now and again on the Kalends
a girlfriend comes to unshutter the gods;
and there's Growler (the puppy) grumbling away—that's some comfort;
she gets to sleep on your side of the bed.
Each little shrine I've draped with flowers;
heaped sacred branches on the crossroad altars;
the incense crackles on ancient hearths.
When the nightowl hoots in a nearby wood,
or the guttering lamp is calling for wine,
that day demands the blood of new born lambs,
and the deacons, tucking up their skirts,
grow hot for gain.

For the glory of storming the heights of Bactra,
and stripping the fine-spun linen from a perfumed general,
is it worth being peppered by sling-shot,
and sniped at by the twanging bow
of a horse in flight? Bring Parthia's sons to heel,
parade in triumph carrying the spear of honour,
but never violate the treaty of my marriage bed.
I want you back—but want you on those terms.
Then I'll dedicate your weapons on the Porta Capena,
and write these words of thanks
FOR LOVE PRESERVED.

TARPEIA

the story of her crime and grisly burial
and how the fortress of ancient Jupiter
fell into enemy hands

There was a sacred grove, in a hollow overhung with ivy,
 thick-wooded, loud with the babble of spring-water;
Sylvanus lived among its branches, and in the heat of the day the music
 of the shepherd's pipe would call the sheep to drink there.
Here Tatius pitched camp, fenced it with stakes of maple-wood,
 and ringed it—for good measure—with a mound of earth.
Those days in Rome, when the people of Cures blew their trumpet,
 you could hear the echoes rumbling on Jupiter's mountain;
and in the Roman Forum, where now we issue judgments
 to lands under our sway, stood Sabine arms.
For walls they had mountains—in place of the senate-house a sheepfold,
 and soldiers brought their horses to drink at that spring.

And there Tarpeia went to fetch water for the goddess,
 balancing a clay water-pot on her head.
(Is it enough, Vesta, for a girl like that to die once,
 a girl who could double-cross your sacred flame?)
Catching sight of Tatius exercising on the open sand,
 (the flash of painted shield on golden mane),
she stood there stunned by the king's beauty, his kingly armour;
 and the pot fell from her unthinking hands.
She'd had signs from the moon, so she said (but the moon wasn't guilty),
 she must go and rinse her hair in the spring-water;
and she prayed to the indulgent nymphs, with gifts of silvery lilies,
 not to let Romulus spoil her Tatius' beauty.

As the smoke was rising on the Capitol from the first fires of evening,
she made her way back, her arms all torn with brambles,
and on the Tarpeian rock she rested, weeping for her wounds
(while Jupiter her neighbour stopped his ears):

"See the camp fires burning, there's Tatius' squadron, there's his tent—
O Sabine weapons beautiful to my eyes
make me your prisoner, let me sit before your household gods—
make me the prisoner of Tatius, and let the world see it.
Good-bye to the mountains of Rome, to Rome built on the mountains,
good-bye to Vesta, object of my shame;
my love is on horseback heading for camp, and the horse he rides on
is groomed for war by the hand of Tatius.
Is it any wonder that Scylla ravaged her father's locks,
and rabid whelps grew from her gleaming loins?
Is it any wonder that Ariadne cheated her monstrous brother
and opened up the maze with a piece of thread?
I will commit a crime for Italian girls to remember:
I served the virgin hearth—and played the whore.
If you're wanting to know why the fire of Pallas has gone out,
forgive me: my tears fell on the altar.
People are saying that the whole city will be drunk tomorrow—
take the path along the ridge through the dewy brambles.
But it's slippery and treacherous going; there's a hidden watercourse
all the way along, and you can't tell where it runs.
If only I knew some magic spells; then I could sing
like Medea to help a handsome lover.
You'd look good in an embroidered toga—better than that changeling
suckled on the tough dugs of a brutish wolf.
Proudly I'd walk a conqueror's queen in my native courtyard,
and it's quite a dowry I'd bring you—Rome betrayed.
Or if not that, then get your revenge for the Sabine women,
take me, abduct me, pay them back in kind.
Marry me and I'll stop the fighting—my bridal gown
can be the mediator in a peace treaty.
Sing out the wedding song, let the harsh trumpets stop their growling;
that marriage bed, believe me, will temper your weapons.
The horn sounds the fourth watch—morning is on its way,

the stars are falling, sinking into the ocean;
I'll try to get to sleep, and I'll look for you in my dreams.
Let your shade come gentle to my eyes."

With these words she yielded her arms to fitful sleep,
not knowing that strange new madness shared her bed;
for the blessed guardian of the embers of Troy, the goddess Vesta
gave fuel to her passion, stoked the fires in her bones,
and drove her wild, like a maenad on the banks of the swift-flowing Thermodon
with her tunic ripped open and her breasts bared.
It was a holiday in the city—our ancestors called it the Parilia—
the anniversary of the building of the walls;
every year the shepherds have a feast, there are games in the city,
and the tables in the villages are soaked in plenty.
There are bonfires of straw dotted around, and crowds of drunken peasants
jump over them with filthy blackened feet.
Romulus gave orders for a day of rest—no guard duty,
no bugle calls—all quiet in the camp.
Tarpeia thought this was her moment, arranged a meeting with the enemy,
and struck a bargain—with herself as one of the terms.
"Take this route; they think it's too steep; and the sentry's on holiday."
He moves fast, slits the dogs' throats before they can bark.
The whole place seems to be asleep—only Jupiter
stays awake to see his sentence executed.
She's opened the gate, betrayed the city as it lies helpless,
and she asks him when the wedding will be—let him name the day.
Now Tatius was our enemy, but he gave her no honor for her wickedness:
"Marry me," he cried, "climb into my royal bed."
And smashed her beneath the shields of his comrades, blow upon blow—
an appropriate dowry for services rendered.

And that's how the rock got its name
from TARPEIA who showed the way
and she the false sentinel
got her reward.

ODE TO A BAWD

May your grave
be choked with thorns

May your shade
be parched with thirst

May your spirit
find no rest

May Cerberus half-starved
howl over your vile bones

She could have turned Hippolytus to sex:
a real pro. Beware you happy lovers
this bird of doom. Why, even Penelope
would have stopped her ears to news of her husband
and married Antinous (he could hardly wait).
Let her but will it
and magnets don't draw iron, birds in their nests
play the stepmother to their fledglings.
A handful of Colline herbs sprinkled in a trench
would wash away the cornfields. Oh she'd not scruple
to lay down the law to the spellbound moon,
or change her skin for a night-prowling wolf.
There's a trick she's got for blinding watchful husbands:
clawing out the eyes of hapless ravens. And just for me
she's consulted the vampires about bloodsucking
and tapped the lymph of a pregnant mare.

She'd work away at her job, wheedling, persistent
like drips of water boring through a rock:

"If Eastern gold be your delight
from the banks of Dorozantian streams
or the shell that lords it under Tyrian waters;
rich fabrics of Cos, tapestries of gossamer
cut from the couches of Attalus, luxury goods
from Thebes where the palm trees grow, porcelain goblets
fired in the kilns of Parthia,

scorn truth,

trample the gods,

let falsehood reign supreme,

break down the laws of chastity (it's bad for business).
Some hints for putting your price up:
tell him you're 'going steady'; find some excuse
for keeping him waiting—love delayed
comes running back the stronger; if he loses his temper
and grabs you by the hair, exploit
his anger, make him sue for peace
on profitable terms; and to cap it all
when you've made the sale and promised delivery,
tell him it's the Isis festival—you've taken the pledge.
Get Iole to drop remarks like 'Fancy,
April already,' while Amycle drives it home
that your birthday's on the Ides of May; just let him sit there
cap in hand, while you go on writing (it doesn't matter what)
sitting in your armchair—little tricks like these
can break his nerve, and then you've got him.
See that there are teeth marks on your neck—fresh ones—
to make him think you've been in some lovers' tangle
and gave as good as you got.
And don't be like Medea, pushful, vindictive,
(You know why she got jilted: she asked first)
but more like Thais in Menander's play
(he was a man of the world), a high-priced harlot
who could outwit the wiles of a Geta. Adjust yourself
to the character of your client; if he wants a sing-song,

then sing along with him, make it a drunken duet.
As for your doorman he should be wide-awake
to customers who pay, but to one who knocks
empty-handed, stone-deaf slumped in sleep
against the bolt. And don't say no to a soldier
just because he's no lover-boy; or a sailor,
so long as there's money in those coarse hands;
or a fellow who once had a price tag
hanging round his savage neck
and jumped in the forum with chalk on his feet.
Keep your eyes on the gold, not on the hand that brings it.
If you listen to poems, all you get is words.
'But what's the use my love' he'll sing
'of walking around like a mannequin
with dolled-up hair
and showing off your sinuous curves
in sheerest silk?'
If it's all poems, and no silk, then stop your ears:
his lyre is bankrupt.
While your life is in the springtime,
and the years are free from wrinkles, make the most of it;
tomorrow may snatch it from your lips. I can remember
in the sweet-smelling gardens of Paestum seeing roses in their prime
lying scorched and withered in the hot winds of morning."

And that's the sort of notions that old Spiny
fills my sweetheart's head with, while I'm reduced
to a bag of bones. O Venus queen of lovers
I've slit the throat of a ringdove at your altar;
accept it as my thankyou. For I saw her
with the phlegm congealing in her shrivelled throat,
the bloody spittle dribbling through the gaps in her teeth,
as she lay gasping out her stinking spirit
on her ancestral mat; and the fire was dead
in her shivering hovel.
And these shall be her exequies:
on her hair (what's left of it) a stolen chaplet,
a faded turban foul with mould,

and a bitch to mourn her (she was always on the lookout
to sink her teeth in my fingers
as I slipped them through the grille.)

And for your burial place

a wine jar
with a broken neck

where the fig tree grows
to crack your bones

and lovers pelt
your tomb with muck

and mingle curses
with the stones.

6 

Hold your peace: a poet is worshipping here.
Let the axe strike and the heifer
fall before my altar. Give me
a garland of Rome to match
the ivy clusters of Philetas,
and let the waters of Cyrene
flow from my lustral urn.
Bring me offerings of soothing
nard and sweet-smelling incense;
three times let the skein of wool
wind round my hearth; sprinkle
my head with water, and on fresh altars
let the ivory flute pour
from Phrygian jars its libation of song.
Away with you, deceit and lies;
let malice breed under an alien
sky: the poet breaks new ground,
but his path is smoothed by the holy laurel.

*

My theme Calliope
is worthy of your blessing:
the temple of Apollo on the Palatine.
To the glory of Caesar I spin my song
and a song about Caesar should make
even Jupiter stop and listen.

*

Running inland to the Athamanes (Apollo's home)
there's an anchorage, a bay,
muffling the roar of Ionian waves,
recalling Actium recalling
that Julian ship, a sea
you might call it, an easy passage
for the prayers of sailors.
Here the world's powers
collided, hulks of timber towered
unbudging on the water (but the birds
were not impartial)
On their left a fleet doomed
by Quirinus of Troy, javelins
in the hands of a woman.
This side Augustus' ship, sails filled
with the blessing of Jupiter, standards
well-versed in national victory.
The lines stood ready bent like bows
drawn by the sea god, armour
glittering on the painted waters
making them tremble;
when Apollo leaving Delos,
now rooted firm by his protection (once
a vagrant driven by the winds' anger),
was there standing a god
over the ship of Augustus, and suddenly
lightning blazed twisting
in a zigzag of flame;
no long hair this time, flowing
over his shoulders, no
tortoise-shell lyre with its gentle music,
but a look like the look he gave
Agamemnon son of Pelops
as he carted away his soldiers to the greedy pyre,
or the time he unwound the Python
slackened her loops and coils for her
(scourge of the gentle muses),
and then he spoke:

                                        Offspring of Alba,
guardian of the world, you, Augustus,
you who have shown yourself greater
than your ancestors, greater than Hector,
now for a sea victory (for the land is already yours)
and my bow fights at your side and the whole
weight of the quiver that hangs from my shoulder.
Set your country free from fear, who leans
on your protection, heaping your prow
with the prayers of a nation. Save her! To what end
did Romulus see those birds flying on the Palatine?
O shameful trespass—galleys of a tyrant lording
over Latin waters in your principate.
You need not fear the hundred oars that wing them
(they glide over a grudging sea), prows
equipped with rock-brandishing centaurs: you'll find them
hollow lumps of wood, bugaboos dressed up in paint.
What makes a soldier fight bravely or breaks his strength
is what he's fighting for; without justice
shame dashes the weapons from his hands.
Now is the moment; let battle begin.
                                                                  And I,
who call the time, will lead your Julian prows
with a hand wreathed in laurel.

And no sooner spoke
        than drawing his bow let fly a quiverful,
                and Caesar's spear came next.
Apollo was good as his word
        Rome conquered, the woman
                got what she deserved, her sceptre
                        broken in pieces carried over Ionian waters.
And father Caesar
        looked down in wonder from his Idalian star:
                I am a god, he said, this day
                        has proved my blood.
Then came Triton blowing his horn,
        and every single goddess of the sea

danced round the standards of freedom
clapping her hands;
while she
headed for the Nile in a tiny boat clinging
to hopes of flight, and all she got for it
was the right to choose her own day for dying.
And gods be thanked;
what sort of a triumph would that be? one woman
(WOMAN) on the selfsame route
where once they dragged Jugurtha.

*

And that's how Apollo got his memorial
for sinking ten ships
with every arrow.

*

Enough of war songs;
Apollo victorious
asks for his lyre back,
strips off his armour
for the dances of peace.
Come dressed in white to the gentle woods, come feasting;
drape my neck with the soft kiss of roses;
let the crushed grape spurt from Falernian presses;
and drench my hair with saffron.
And may the Muses
inflame the genius of poets drunk (for Bacchus
is a source of inspiration to his friend Apollo)
to sing the subjugation
of bog-dwelling Sygambri;
of Meroe and the dusky kingdoms;
of how the Parthians owned up at last
and made a treaty:
"It's Roman standards this time, soon they'll be giving their own.
And anything Augustus spares those Eastern bowmen,
let him save it as a trophy for his sons.

Rejoice Crassus if you have any consciousness
lying in those dark sands:
the Euphrates lies open
and the road to your burial place."

And I'll make a night of it
pouring libations of wine
and song
till the morning fills my glass with sunlight.

So death is not the end of it; ghosts
exist, pale wraiths flitting
from the inconclusive pyre.

I saw Cynthia leaning over my pillow; they'd just buried her
by the highway's edge (you could hear the traffic passing);
sleep was slow coming after the funeral; my bed
was a cold untenanted kingdom—and there she stood;
no change in her hairstyle from when they carried her off,
no change in her eyes, but her dress
was charred to her body, and the ring on her finger
(beryl as usual) eaten by the flames, her lips shrivelled
by the waters of Lethe. And yet her voice and her temper
were very much alive, as she snapped her bony fingers at me:

You cheat, you hypocrite (yet that's the best
that a woman can hope for) how can you sleep
so soon? Had you forgotten
our night games on the Subura
(nobody slept there) those subterfuges
that wore a track across my window ledge:
there I was, dangling on a rope
lowering myself, hand over hand,
into your arms. We used to make love then
on street corners, twining
our bodies together, while our cloaks
took the chill off the sidewalk.
So much for our secret compact—lies,
empty words blown to pieces
by the unheeding winds.

There was nobody to cry my name as my eyes grew dim
(a call from you would have won me a day's respite)
nobody to keep guard over me rattling his castanets
(so I got my head cut by a broken tile).
Where were you at my funeral pyre? did anyone see you
hunched with grief, bathing your black toga
with your hot tears? Too much trouble, was it,
to go beyond the city gate? You might at least have asked them
to carry me slowly that far. But why weren't you there
praying for winds, scenting the flames with spikenard?
A handful of cheap hyacinths, a wine jar
duly broken over my ashes—
would that have been too much to ask?

Heat up the branding irons, and burn
the truth out of Lygdamus: that wine was spiked
with the taint of death. And Nomas can hide away
her mysterious juices, but a red-hot brick
will make that old witch talk. And look at this one
trailing the hem of her golden gown; once
she was open to the public at cheap nightly rates.
Now any girl who's careless enough
to say that I was beautiful
gets an extra load of wool in her basket. Poor old Petale
put a garland on my tomb and for her pains
got hobbled by a filthy clog. And Lalage
was strung up by her hair and given the lash
for asking a favour—and mentioning my name.
And you just watched while she melted down
my golden statue, putting me to the flames
to win herself a dowry.

But I haven't come here to attack you, Propertius,
though I must say you deserve it. All those years
that I reigned as queen of your verses; and I swear
by the song of Fate that no man may unravel,
by the threefold dog (and may his bark be gentle)
that I have been faithful. May vipers if I lie

hiss in my tomb and build their nests
over my bones.

There are two destinations
beyond that hateful river; two separate routes
for the rowboats of the numberless dead.
One way goes leching Clytemnestra, Pasiphae
with her mimic cow, that wooden obscenity.
But look there are others sped on their way
in a boat that's crowned with garlands
where the joyful breezes kiss
the roses of Elysium
and the lute makes music and the cymbals
clash and the turbaned dancers
whirl to the Lydian lyre.
And there Andromeda and Hypermestre,
brave hearts, wives without taint,
tell their famous stories; one laments
for arms bruised by a mother's chains, hands clinging
to icy cliffs she hadn't earned, while Hypermestre tells
of the monstrous thing her sisters did, a crime
she hadn't got the heart for. We weep in death
to heal the loves of a lifetime. And I keep to myself
the record of your infidelities.

No, I came to give some instructions, if you're still in a mood
to listen, not yet totally hooked
by the spells of Chloris. First, there's my old nanny
Parthenie; don't let her want for anything
in her trembling years; she kept an open door for you
and never charged admission. And my darling Valette (a good name
for a lady's maid), may she never have to hold up the looking glass
to a new mistress. And those poems you wrote about me,
I want you to burn them, all of them; it's time you stopped
living off my praises.

And on my grave let ivy grow
in swelling clusters gently wreathing my bones
with its tangled hair. Where Anio rich in apples
broods on the wooded meadows, and the power of Hercules

keeps ivory gleaming, write this poem on my tombstone
for all to see (it does me justice, and it's short enough
for the traveller from town to read it as he passes);

HERE IN THE FIELDS OF TIVOLI
LIES GOLDEN CYNTHIA
ADDING A NEW GLORY
TO THE BANKS OF THE ANIO

Listen! there is a meaning in dreams
that come through the holy gate; do not scorn
dreams that are holy. We are night wanderers, night
unbolts the prisonhouse of the shades, and Cerberus
is on the prowl; with the light of morning, law
demands our return to Lethe's pools.
We climb on board, and the ferryman
takes a roll-call of his cargo.

For the time being
I leave you to other women, soon
you'll be all mine, to hold and to crush
in a jumble of bones."

As soon as she had finished
her business with me, with its tone
of bitter accusation, her shade
slipped from my encircling arms.

8 

Let me tell you about last night's alarms
and excursions on the Esquiline; folk
came running to the scene in swarms
from the whole neighbourhood round the park.
There was a brawl in a backstreet dive, a donnybrook
that filled the air with shouting and cursing.
And though I wasn't there in person,
it's my reputation that will bear the mark.

The town of Lanuvium has long been guarded
by an ancient serpent; the place is worth a stop:
it's an unusual sight, and your time will be rewarded.
There's a black hole that leads down to the shrine by a sheer drop;
this is the point of entry (best avoided
by virgins) for the offering of cake
demanded every year by the hungry snake
writhing and hissing in his underground keep.

Young girls perform the rite; fear drains the blood
from their faces as they go down to the appalling gamble
of those snaky jaws, that snatch the scraps of food
they offer, and make the very baskets tremble
in the poor girls' hands; those with their maidenhood
still intact come back safe and sound
to their parents' arms; and the farmers' cries resound:
"This year the crops will be good!"

And it's there that Cynthia went, driving
a team of ponies, elegantly clipped, on a visit
(so she said) to Juno, though the goddess she was serving
sounded more like Venus. You saw it, Appia, how was it?

that magnificent procession, the pomp
of chariot wheels hurtling across your paving,
and she, (what a sight!) crouched over the pole, swerving
like a demon into every pothole and bump.

As for that smoothskinned fop I'd rather not speak
about him, with his fashionable carriage
all draped in silk, the bracelets round the neck
of his Molossian dogs. One day
he'll have to sell his own life to pay
for a plate of gladiatorial porridge
when a beard (Oh horrors!) forces its obscene way
over his depilated cheek.

As this was by no means the first occasion
I'd been cheated of a bed I thought was mine,
I decided to strike camp, move down the line
and set up a new base for operation.
There's a girl I know called Phyllis, she's a neighbour
of the goddess Diana on the Aventine,
not much to recommend her when sober,
but she's quite charming with a little wine.

Then there's Teia, who lives close to the Tarpeian
grove—a pretty girl, but when she's in liquor
she isn't satisfied with just one man.
So I asked them over to make the night pass quicker
(also because I hoped to introduce
some variety into my love life). On a patch of green
stood a couch, well concealed, just for the three of us
to lie on. If you wondered, I was in between.

Lygdamus served the wine, using the glass chalice
I keep for summer; we had an excellent
vintage from Methymna; the Nile sent
a flute player; and Phyllis
brought her castanets; and there were roses, ready
for strewing, in all their guileless

elegance; while Brobdignag with dwarfish body
and stumpy fingers beat time to the flute solos.

But everything went wrong: the flame kept trembling
though I'd filled the lamp, the table legs
collapsed, and when I tried for Love by gambling
all I got was those bloody dogs.*
I didn't see their naked breasts, I was deaf
when they sang to me; far away, rambling
by the gates of Lanuvium, all by myself—
when suddenly there came a distant rumbling.

It was the creaking of door hinges I heard first,
and the hum of voices by the entrance hall,
but it wasn't long before Cynthia burst
in, flattening the doors against the wall,
with her hair unkempt, but beautiful
in the wildness of her fury; and the cup slipped
from my paralysed fingers, my jaw dropped
and my wine-stained lips grew pale.

Her eyes flashed like thunderbolts; she was savage
as a woman could be; the scene as dramatic
as the sacking of a city: Phyllis with her face ravaged
by those furious fingernails, Teia in a panic
screaming "Fire! Fire!" to the neighbourhood. The frantic
brandishing of torches soon awoke
the local citizenry—and the whole block
resounded to our midnight antics.

With their hair torn out in handfuls, great rips
in their tunics, off they blunder
to the nearest pub; rejoicing in her plunder
Cynthia comes running back, victorious, and slaps
my face with a stinging backhand blow,
sinks her teeth in my neck till the blood drips,

*The reference is to dicing, where the highest throw was called "Venus" and the lowest "canes" or "the dogs."

and my eyes (as specially deserving to take the rap)
she beats till they're black and blue.

She kept up the barrage as long as her arms could bear it;
then she hauled Lygdamus out of his niche
under the left-hand headboard of the couch.
He grovelled there praying to my guardian Spirit.
But I couldn't help you, Lygdamus; I was as much
a prisoner as you. So I sued for terms
desperately throwing my suppliant arms,
around the feet she'd hardly let me touch.

"If what you want is a pardon for your crime,
then here are my conditions" she said: "there's to be no
strolling all dressed up in Pompey's portico,
ambling through the sandy forum at circus-time,
craning your neck in the theatre to look at the back row,
hanging around staring into open litters;
and above all no Lygdamus—he'll have to go;
put him up for sale, clamp him in double fetters."

I accepted her conditions as stated.
She laughed, enjoying her sense of power, then douched
the doorstep with clean water, and fumigated
anything those interlopers had touched.
She had the oil changed in the lamps, singed my head
three times with sulphur, then started
changing the blankets; I cooperated;
and we laid down our weapons all over the bed.

9 

AMPHITRYONIADES
driving the oxen from their pasturage
in Erythea, came to the unvanquishable
hills, the sheep-cropped Palatine,
and there rested (he and his cattle
each as tired as the other) by the pools
of VELABRUM—a real river then, sail-studded
(veliferous) in the centre of the city.
But they didn't stay safe long, not with
Cacus for their host, desecrating
Jupiter with cattle theft. (Cacus
was a local brigand, his den was a fearsome
cave, and he had three mouths
each with its own voice). To leave
no sign of the theft, tail first
he dragged them backwards into the cave.
But the god gave witness: the lowing of oxen
cried "thief," and the thief's implacable
door was smashed in anger.
His three heads beaten in
by that famous club, Cacus
lay dead. "Go, my oxen," said Alcides,
"go, oxen of Hercules, fruits
of my last labour, twice sought, twice
won, go my oxen, feed
on these fields and christen them
with your interminable lowing the OX-
MEADOWS—one day to be famous
as a forum of Rome."
                                        And when he had spoken
his throat was parched, his lips

tormented by thirst, but not a drop flowed
from the fecund earth. Far off
behind a wall he heard the laughter
of girls; there was a clearing ringed
by shady trees, the private places
of the Bona Dea, a holy spring
no man may touch unpunished.
There was a lonely entrance hung
with purple fillets; a temple
with its crumbling beams reeking
of the flare of incense, decorated
by the long fingers of a popular tree,
the birds singing deep
within its shade. Here Hercules
came running (dust clogged
his dry beard) and hurled before the entrance
these ungodlike words: "Help me!
you who play in this sacred
arbour, open your shrine
to a man that is weary. Water!
I need water; all around me
I hear the babble of springs—
just let me scoop it in my cupped
hands and drink.

Haven't you heard
of the man who carried the world on his shoulders?
I am he, Alcides—that's what the earth
I rescued calls me. Haven't you heard
of the brave deeds of Hercules' club, the weapons
that always struck home against monsters,
and how the darkness of Styx grew light
for one man only? Now I have come
to this neck of the world, still dragging
my destiny behind me; grudgingly
this land opens its arms
to my weariness; and though this were Juno's
temple, and you were her priestesses, even she

my stepmother wouldn't be cruel enough
to bar me from her waters. Is it my face
that frightens you, or the rough lion skin
or my hair charred by the Libyan sun?
Once I served as a maid in a Tyrian
dress, spinning on a Lydian
distaff; with a soft stomacher
to bind my shaggy breast,
I did well as a girl, in spite of
my horny hands."

But the kindly old
priestess, her white hair wreathed
with threads of purple, answered:
"Keep away, stranger, spare
your eyes, flee this awesome
grove; it is not safe for a man
to come near this altar in the seclusion
of its tiny temple; it is protected
by a dreadful interdict. Think
of the price Tiresias paid
for seeing Pallas, her Gorgon
shield laid aside, bathing
her warrior limbs. God grant you
other springs; these sequestered
streams flow in their sacred channel
for girls alone."

But Hercules
beat down the shady doorposts
with his shoulders; the bolts gave
before the fury of his thirst; he drained
the river, cooled his burning throat,
and with the water still on his lips, pronounced
this grim decree:

"May the ARA
MAXIMA, mightiest of altars,
to be built by these hands in thanks
for the recovery of my cattle, never

be open for girls to worship at,
so the thirst of Hercules may be avenged
in perpetuity."

The Sabines built him
a temple and called him SANCUS
for cleansing the world and sanctifying it.
Hail father (beloved now
even of cruel Juno) hail
SANCUS! May you graciously accept
this place in my poems.

JUPITER FERETRIUS
the origin of his name and of his temple
three sets of armour from three chieftains won

That's a massive peak to scale,
but the prospect of glory gives me strength,
and what's the pleasure in picking garlands
where the slopes are easy?

It was you Romulus who pioneered this prize—
well-stocked with spoils you came back from the foe,
when Acron the Sabine made for the city gates,
and you sprawled him over the body of his horse
with your victorious spear; Acron, of the breed of Hercules,
leader from the fortress at Caenina, scourge
of the fields of Rome in days gone by, aspired
in his folly to strip the spoils from Quirinus' shoulders,
but it was he who did the giving, and it was his blood
that dripped from them. Romulus, seeing him with weapons poised
against the hollow towers, preempted him
with a prayer that came true: "Jupiter, here is your victim;
today Acron will fall before your feet." He made his vow,
Acron fell, and Jupiter received his spoils.
Father of our city, founder of our courage, he was an old hand
at victory; his hard upbringing had trained him
to stand the cold; he was a horseman with as much skill
at the plough as the bridle; he wore a bushy-plumed helmet
of wolf skin, no gaudy bronze-bespangled shield,
but a tough belt made of plain cow-leather.

And next came Cossus, who killed Tolumnius of Veii—
in those days conquering Veii was no easy matter:
the sound of war had not yet crossed the Tiber;
Nomentum and Cora (with its three acres per man)
were our most distant spoils. Ancient Veii,
what a kingdom you were then with your golden throne
set up in the marketplace. Now the leisurely music
of the shepherd's horn sounds within your walls,
and over your bones they go harvesting. The leader
was standing on a tower above the gate parleying
without fear on his own home ground, while the brazen-horned ram
kept up its steady battering on the walls
under the shelter of its long mantle. "Brave men" said Cossus
"should fight in the open." At once both champions stood
facing each other on the plain. The gods gave victory
to Latin hands, and the severed head of Tolumnius
bathed with its blood the horses of Rome.

Claudius beat off an enemy from beyond the Rhine
and brought home with him the Belgian shield of their leader
the gigantic Virdomarus, offspring (so he boasted)
of the Rhine itself; he was famous for the way
he dashed forward in his chariot scattering his Gallic javelins;
but this time as he moved out in front of the line, dressed
in his striped breeches, Claudius hacked off his head
and the horseshoe ring fell from his neck.

So now there are three sets of spoils
        stored in this temple—
        FERETRIUS they call it
since leader STRUCK leader and the gods gave blessing;
or else it's because these arms were CARRIED home
        on conquering shoulders
that this stately altar got the name
        of JUPITER FERETRIUS.

11 

It's no use, Paullus, badgering my tomb
with lamentations. The black gate of death
opens to no entreaties. When the dead have come
within hell's jurisdiction, the upward path
stands blocked with unrelenting adamant.

And all your tears will run into the sand.
Perhaps the god that rules in that dim court
would hear your plea, but the indifferent shores
hear nothing. Keep your prayers
for the gods above: once the ferryman
has pocketed his fare, the pallid door clangs shut
on the world of shadows.
That is the mournful tune
the trumpet played as the malignant flame
licked round my bier and dragged my soul to rest.
Marriage to a Paullus, the triumphal chariot
of my ancestors, the living testimonies of my fame
could do nothing to soften Cornelia's fate.
And I am become a handful of dust.

Darkness of hell, you swamps and stagnant pools
and all the waters that wind round my feet,
though I come before my time, I am without guilt—
may father Dis deal gently with my soul.

Or if there's an Aeacus sitting on the judgment throne
with the urn at his side, let him judge my case
when my name is called, with his brothers to give advice,
and next to Minos the grim-faced platoon
of the Eumenides keeping watch

over the hushed assembly.

Sisyphus, forget your stone;

today may the lips of Tantalus catch
the teasing waters; the wheels of Ixion grind to a halt;
and savage Cerberus leave the shades alone,
his chain hanging loose from the silent bolt.

I speak in my own defence; and if I lie
may I be condemned to suffer the same fate
as the Danaid sisters, my shoulders crushed beneath the weight
of that unhappy urn.

If any one has ever claimed glory

for the trophies of their ancestors, then so can I:
for the names of my grandfathers tell the story
of Africa and Numantia; the Libones on my mother's side
stand as their equals; each house is pillared high
by the record of its services.

So much for my birth.

When the time came to lay aside
the purple toga for the marriage torch
and bind my tresses with a different coif,
I gave myself then, Paullus, to your couch,
and nothing could make me leave it, nothing but death.
Write on my tomb that I have been one man's wife.

Ashes of my ancestors, objects of Rome's reverence,
beneath whose conquests Africa lies crushed,
and Perses, that would-be Achilles, with his whole house smashed
Achilles and all, I call you in evidence
that my life has been without taint, no fault of mine
has weakened the censor's law, or made your fireside blush.

Cornelia has done nothing to diminish
the glory of that house; she herself has been
part of its greatness. Between
the torch of marriage and the torch of death,
I have lived nobly and without sin.

The conscience nature gave me at my birth
was stronger than any fear of being punished.

So do with me as you will, I shall not fear
your verdict; though Claudia, handmaid of Cybele,
who took a rope and dragged the goddess clear
to show that she was chaste, or she whose dress caught fire
on the sacred altar and gave Vesta back her flame
should sit with me in court, they would feel no shame.

Call Scribonia to the witness stand:
My darling mother, have I not been good
to you, is there anything you would want changed in me
except my fortune? A mother's tears and the grief
of a whole city are my eulogy.
Call Caesar next; for we have seen the god
in tears for the death of one who in her life
was a sister to his daughter and a worthy friend.

Twice has my brother sat on the chair of state.
Death took me from him in his consulship.
And I have honours too, that outlive the rape
of death, children in my house, the proud prize
of a mother. Lepidus and Paullus, my sons, my hope,
you held me in your arms and closed my eyes.

And you my daughter, fair advertisement
of your father's censorship, imitate
your mother, be faithful to one man.
My children, may you have children of your own;
they are the pillars of a house. I shall be content
when my boat leaves shore knowing my life lives on
in them. This is a woman's triumph, her ultimate
reward: to live in the praises on her children's lips.

Paullus, I give the children to your care,
the pledges of the love we shared together.

A mother's feelings do not die, they are burned deep
in my ashes. But it is you who must be mother
and father to them now, it is your neck
they will cling to, your shoulders that will bear the weight
of the whole family. When you kiss away their tears,
kiss them for me.

If you have cause to weep,
don't let them see it, let your cheek be dry
and fool their kisses. You can lie awake
and wear away the night grieving for me;
you can conjure up my image in your sleep
and whisper secrets. But remember when you speak
to speak as one expecting a reply.

Maybe the time will come when the door must face
another marriage bed, and where I was once
there'll be a stepmother sitting warily. My sons
bear with your father, accept her in my place.
She will surrender to your gentleness.
And don't praise your mother too much: comparisons
are invidious and will give offense.

If he remains faithful to the memory
of my shade, and even after my death
I am dear to him, you must learn to see
old age approaching, and leave no path
open for the brooding of a lonely widower.
May you be given the years that were taken from me;
and may his old age be happy in the children I bore.

It has gone well with me: I never wore
a mother's mourning; nobody was missing
at my funeral.

My case is stated, let the court rise
in tears, and the grateful earth grant me its blessing.
A life of virtue reaches to the skies:
may your verdict be, that when I make the crossing
my bones shall be carried to the honoured shore.

GLOSSARY OF NAMES

This glossary should not be the last word. Propertius' allusions, mythological, historical, geographical, should be left open-ended, as they were by the poet. A hint from the poet could lead his Roman reader into the world of myth, a world rich in associations, where the reader could find his own way. To fix his itinerary by definition and selection is a denial of this poetic method. Still, there is no alternative; that world is no longer accessible to us except by such artificial means. All I can do is to ask the reader not to be satisfied with these thumb-nail sketches, but to pursue the references further by all means at his disposal: and to recognise that Propertius' use of allusion is an organic part of his poetic method, not a tiresome and pedantic convention that can be disposed of by brief notes at the end of the book.

I have not considered it necessary to include names that are generally well known (e.g. Homer, The Nile), or those about which nothing is known beyond what we are told by the poems themselves (e.g. Lygdamus, Lycinna).

ACANTHUS 3.9. A plant (bear's-foot) frequently used as a decorative motif in works of art.

ACHELOUS 2.34. A river of northern Greece. As a river god, he was wounded by Hercules in a fight over a woman, Deianira.

ACHERON 3.5. One of the rivers of the underworld.

ACHILLES 2.1,2.3,2.8,2.9a,2.13b,2.22a,3.18,4.11. Son of Peleus and the sea goddess Thetis. The greatest Greek warrior in the Trojan War; when his slave-girl, Briseis, was taken from him by Agamemnon, he retired from the fighting in anger; his close friend Patroclus went into battle wearing his armour and was killed by Hector. To avenge the death of Patroclus, Achilles reentered the battle and killed Hector. He met his death at the hands of Paris by means of an arrow in the heel, the only part of his body that was not invulnerable. Polyxena, youngest daughter of Priam, was sacrificed on his tomb after the sack of Troy.

ACRON 4.10. A king of Caenina (a Sabine town of Latium), who was killed by Romulus in the war that resulted from the Rape of the Sabines (see

Sabines). Romulus dedicated his armour in the Temple of Jupiter Feretrius. This was the first example of the winning of the *Spolia Opima,* a general's reward for killing his opposite number.

ACTIUM 2.1,2.15,2.16,2.34,3.11,4.6. In Epirus on the Ambracian Gulf; site of a naval battle in 31 B.C. where Octavian (later Augustus) defeated Antony and Cleopatra.

ADONIS 2.13b. A beautiful youth, loved by Venus, torn apart by a wild boar when hunting, and changed by Venus into a flower.

ADRASTUS 2.34. One of the Seven against Thebes. Hercules gave him a talking horse called Arion. *See* Archemorus.

AEACUS 4.11. Son of Jupiter and Aegina, celebrated for his piety. After his death he became a judge among the dead.

AEGEAN SEA 1.6,3.7. The sea that lies between the east coast of Greece and Asia Minor.

AEMILIUS 3.3. L. Aemilius Paullus, who conquered Perses, king of Macedon, in 168 B.C. He won an enormous amount of booty and reentered Rome by sailing up the Tiber from the sea.

AESCHYLUS 2.34. Famous Attic tragedian (525–456 B.C.) noted for the grandiose and high-flown nature of his language.

AENEAS 2.34,3.4,4.1. Son of Anchises and Venus. He escaped from the sack of Troy with his father and son Iulus, and carried the gods of Troy to Italy. He was regarded as the founder of the Roman nation.

AGAMEMNON 2.14a,3.18,4.1.ii,4.6. King of Mycenae, leader of the Greek expedition against Troy, brother of Menelaus. When his fleet was becalmed at Aulis, he sacrificed his daughter Iphigenia to secure favourable winds, on the instructions of the prophet Calchas. On his return from Troy he was murdered by his wife Clytemnestra. *See also* Argynnus.

AJAX 4.1. A Greek hero in the Trojan War, who raped the prophet Cassandra at the altar of Athene.

ALBA 3.3,4.1,4.6. Alba Longa (mod. Castel Gandolfo), a town in the Alban Hills, 12 miles southeast of Rome. According to legend it was founded by the son of Aeneas (Iulus or Ascanius) in 1152 B.C.; in fact it was probably only a few decades older than Rome herself.

ALBAN LAKE 3.22. (mod. Lago di Albano) A lake in Latium, south of Rome, near the town of Alba.

ALCIDES 1.20,4.9. Grandson of Alceus, (i.e., Hercules).

ALCINOUS 1.14. King of the Phaeacians in Scheria, father of Nausicaa, visited by Ulysses. His people lived a life of blissful ease and he himself had great wealth; particularly noted for the gardens and orchards surrounding his palace.

ALCMAEON 3.5. Son of Amphiaraus. After the expedition of the Seven against Thebes, he killed his mother Eriphyle to avenge his father. As a result he was pursued by Furies. He married Alphesiboea, but later abandoned her for Callirhoe. The brothers of Alphesiboea killed him for this, and were in turn (according to the Propertius version) killed by their sister.

ALCMENA 2.22a. Wife of Amphitryon; mother of Hercules by Jupiter. Jupiter visited Alcmena assuming the appearance of Amphitryon, and arranged for a night of twice the normal length, arresting the movements of the heavenly bodies.

ALEXANDRIA 3.11. An important city of Egypt founded by Alexander the Great.

ALEXIS 2.34. A shepherd in Vergil's *Eclogues* loved by Corydon.

ALPHESIBOEA 1.15. See Alcmaeon.

AMAZONS 3.14. A tribe of female warriors who lived in Pontus. *See* Hippolyte.

AMPHIARAUS 2.34,3.13. One of the Seven against Thebes. A prophet, he knew he would be killed if he joined the expedition against Thebes, so he hid in his house. His wife Eriphyle was bribed by a golden necklace to give him away. He went to Thebes where he was swallowed up, chariot and all, by a chasm in the earth.

AMPHION 1.9,3.15. Son of Jupiter and Antiope (q.v.) and a famous musician. Together with his brother Zethus he built the walls of Thebes, drawing the stones from Mount Cithaeron with the music of his lyre. He married Niobe.

AMPHITRYONIADES 4.9. A name for Hercules. Amphitryon was his putative, or mortal, father.

AMYMONE 2.26c. Daughter of Danaus. She was raped by Neptune at Lerna in the Argolid while looking for water. Neptune struck the ground with his trident and a spring arose which bore her name.

ANDROGEON 2.1. Son of Minos of Crete, slain by the people of Athens and Megara (for which offence Minos made war on them—see Minos and Scylla). According to Propertius he was restored to life by Asclepius, god of healing; this version of the story is not found elsewhere.

ANDROMACHE 2.20,2.22a. Wife of Hector (there is a famous farewell scene in *Iliad* 6). After the fall of Troy she became the slave of Neoptolemus.

ANDROMEDA 1.3,2.28,3.22,4.7. An Ethiopian princess. Her mother Cassiope boasted that she was more beautiful than the Nereids (sea goddesses). As a punishment, Neptune sent a monster to ravage the land. On the instruction of an oracle Andromeda was chained to a rock and exposed to the monster. Here she was found by Perseus who rescued her by slaying the monster.

ANIO 1.20,3.22,4.7. (mod. Aniene) A tributary of the Tiber, famous for its waterfalls at Tibur (Tivoli).

ANTAEUS 3.22. A Libyan giant, son of Neptune and Earth, who drew his strength from contact with Earth. Hercules defeated him in a wrestling match by holding him up in the air.

ANTIGONE 2.8. Daughter of Oedipus of Thebes. When her brothers, Eteocles and Polynices, fought over the kingdom of Thebes and were both slain, Antigone refused to obey the order of her uncle Creon that Polynices should remain unburied. For her offence she was imprisoned in an underground cave where she hanged herself; Creon's son Haemon, her betrothed, stabbed himself over her body.

ANTIMACHUS 2.34. An epic poet from Colophon (fl. 400 B.C.). He also wrote love poetry to his mistress Lyde. Apparently his suit was not successful

ANTINOUS 4.5. The foremost of Penelope's suitors during the absence of Ulysses.

ANTIOPE 1.4,3.15. Daughter of the River Asopus. She was loved by Jupiter by whom she had two sons, Amphion and Zethus. Imprisoned by Dirce (the reasons given for this vary; in 3.15 the version is that Dirce suspects that she has had an affair with her husband Lycus), she escaped and was recognised and protected by her sons, who put Dirce and Lycus to death.

AONIAN 3.3. Aonia is the region of Boeotia which includes Mount Helicon. The term does service as a general epithet of the Muses.

APELLES 1.2,3.9. A famous painter of the 4th century B.C. from Colophon in Asia Minor. One of his most famous paintings was the Birth of Venus.

APHRODITE 3.13. The Greek goddess of love (Latin Venus). "Aphrodite's Shell" refers to pearl or mother-of-pearl.

APOLLO 3.2,3.9,3.11,4.1,4.6. The god of the arts, medicine, archery and prophecy; son of Jupiter and Latona (Leto); born on the island of Delos. There was a temple of Apollo at Actium which was restored after Augustus' victory in 31 B.C. Augustus also dedicated a temple to Apollo on the Palatine in 28 B.C. His most important oracle was at Delphi. He is known also as Phoebus, the shining one.

APPIAN WAY 2.32,4.8. The most important road of southern Italy, running from Rome to Naples; started in 312 B.C. by Appius Claudius.

ARA MAXIMA 4.9. An altar in the Forum Boarium in Rome, supposed to have been founded by Hercules. Women were not allowed to take part in worship there.

ARATUS 2.34. A Greek poet from Soli in Cilicia (fl. 250 B.C.); best known for his didactic poem on astronomy called *Phenomena* which was translated by Cicero.

ARAXES 4.3. (mod. Aras) A river in Armenia flowing into the Caspian Sea.

ARCHEMORUS 2.34. A child nursed by Hypsipyle. When the Seven came to Nemea on their way to Thebes, Hypsipyle showed them where to find water; while she was doing this the child was killed by a snake. The Nemean Games were instituted for Archemorus's funeral, and Adrastus' horse, Arion, ridden by Polynices, won a victory in the games.

ARCHYTAS 4.1.ii. A distinguished mathematician and astronomer from Tarentum, who lived in the first half of the 4th century B.C.; he was visited by Plato.

ARGANTHUS 1.20. A mountain in Mysia, near Bithynia.

ARGO 1.20,2.24,2.26c,3.22. The ship in which the Argonauts travelled to Colchis (reputed to be the first ship ever built). In the course of their journey they had to pass through the Clashing Rocks (Symplegades); they succeeded in doing this by sending a dove through first to see how long the rocks remained open.

ARGUS 1.3. A many-eyed monster. Juno gave him the task of watching over Io, Jupiter's mistress, whom she had turned into a heifer. Later he was killed by Mercury on the orders of Jupiter.

ARGYNNUS 3.7. A Boeotian boy with whom Agamemnon fell in love when the Greek fleet was at Aulis. He was drowned in the River Cephisus and buried by Agamemnon. The passage in 3.7 suggests that Agamemnon missed an opportunity to sail because of this, which in turn led to the sacrifice of Iphigenia.

ARIADNE 1.3,2.3,2.14a,2.24,3.17,4.4. Daughter of Minos of Crete and Pasiphae. She fell in love with Theseus, helped him to slay the Minotaur and find his way out of the Labyrinth by means of a thread, and fled with Theseus but was abandoned by him on the Island of Naxos. There she was found by Bacchus who eventually translated her to the stars as a constellation.

ARION 2.26a. A famous poet and lute player from Methymna (fl. 625 B.C.). He is said to have been thrown overboard by sailors as he was en route from Sicily to Corinth, but to have been rescued and carried to shore by a dolphin. (Arion was also the name of Adrastus' talking horse. *See* Adrastus and Archemorus).

ASCANIUS 1.20. A lake in Bithynia.

ASCRA 2.34. A village in Boeotia; birthplace of the poet Hesiod.

ASSISI 4.12. A hill town in Umbria, possibly the birthplace of Propertius.

ATALANTA 1.1. A virgin huntress from Arcadia resembling Artemis in many respects. She was wooed and won by Milanion (q.v.).

ATHAMANES 4.6. The inhabitants of Athamania, a district of Epirus in northern Greece.

ATLAS 3.22. A giant, identified with the mountains of that name in North Africa. He carried the sky on his shoulders. He offered to fetch the apples of the Hesperides for Hercules if Hercules carried the sky meanwhile; he then refused to take back the burden until he was forced.

ATRIDES 3.7. Son of Atreus, i.e., Agamemnon or Menelaus.

ATTALUS 4.5. King of Pergamum in Asia Minor, 269–197 B.C.; said to have invented the art of weaving cloth of gold.

AUGUSTUS 2.10,3.11,4.6. The title given to Octavian, grand nephew and adoptive son of Julius Caesar, in 27 B.C. As *Princeps* or chief citizen, he became to all intents sole ruler of the Roman Empire till his death in 14 A.D. All future emperors adopted this title.

AULIS 3.7,4.1.i. A port in Boeotia where the Greek fleet assembled before setting out for Troy. It was here that Agamemnon sacrificed his daughter Iphigenia in order to get a favourable wind.

AURORA 2.18a. The goddess of the dawn, daughter of Hyperion, wife of Tithonus, mother of Memnon.

AUSTER 2.26c. The south wind.

AVENTINE 4.1.i,4.8. One of the hills of Rome.

AVERNUS 1.11,3.18,4.1.i. A lake near Puteoli (mod. Pozzuoli, near Naples) reputed to be an entrance to the underworld. It was extremely deep, heavily wooded, and gave off mephitic vapours.

BABYLON 3.11. Ancient city on the Euphrates, traditionally built (or rebuilt) by Queen Semiramis.

BACCHUS 1.3,2.30b,3.2,3.17,4.1,4.2,4.6. Son of Jupiter and Semele, the princess of Thebes. Semele asked to see Jupiter in all his glory and as a result was burnt to ashes; the unborn child was saved and sewn into the thigh of Jupiter. Bacchus was a fertility god, god of wine, the looser of cares, inspirer of poets; he was worshipped in orgiastic rites by a train of maenads or Bacchae; he is usually represented with fawnskin, thyrsus, ivy, and long hair.

BACTRA 3.1,3.11,4.3. The chief city of Bactria, an area which now takes in northern Afghanistan and part of Turkestan.

BAIAE 1.11,1.20,3.18. A fashionable tourist resort on the coast of Campania, famous for its warm baths. M. Claudius Marcellus, nephew of Augustus and earmarked as a possible successor, died here in 23 B.C.; his death is lamented in 3.18.

BASSARID 3.17. Belonging to Bassareus, another name for Bacchus.

BELLEROPHON 3.3. With the help of Athene, he caught and tamed Pegasus, the winged horse.

BOEBE 2.2. Lake Boebis (mod. Karla) in Thessaly.

BONA DEA 4.9. A Roman goddess worshipped only by women.

BOOTES 3.5. A constellation represented as the driver of the Wagon or Plough.

BOSPORUS 3.11. The strait that separates Europe from Asia, running from the Black Sea into the Propontis. The reference in 3.11 is to Pompey's defeat of Mithridates, king of Pontus.

BOVILLAE 4.1. A small town in Latium, colony of Alba Longa, 12 miles from Rome.

BRENNUS 3.13. A Gallic leader who invaded Greece in 279 B.C.; he attacked Delphi and was driven back by thunder, lightning, and an avalanche.

BRIMO 2.2. A name for Persephone, or Hecate, goddess of the underworld.

BRISEIS 2.8,2.9,2.20,2.22a. Slave girl of Achilles, taken from him by Agamemnon, restored after the death of Patroclus.

BRUTUS 4.1.i. Lucius Junius Brutus. He expelled Tarquinius Superbus (*see* Tarquin) and established the Roman Republic. He became consul in 509 B.C.

CACUS 4.9. A monstrous three-headed brigand who lived on the Palatine. He was killed by Hercules for stealing from him the cattle of Geryon.

CADMUS 3.9,3.13. Son of Agenor, King of Tyre; founded Thebes; introduced writing into Greece. Among his children were Ino and Semele.

CAENINA 4.10. A small town of great antiquity in Latium. See Acron.

CALAIS 1.20. Son of Boreas, the north wind. With his brother Zetes, he took part in the expedition of the Argonauts.

CALAMIS 3.9. A Greek sculptor (c. 480–450 B.C.) noted particularly for his horses.

CALCHAS 4.1.ii. A prophet who accompanied the Greeks to Troy; it was he who instructed Agamemnon to sacrifice his daughter Iphigenia at Aulis.

CALLIMACHUS 2.1,2.34,3.1,3.9,4.1.i. A famous Greek poet (fl. 250 B.C.) who was born in Cyrene and lived in Alexandria. Propertius sees himself as the Roman Callimachus, the first to rival in the Latin tongue his elegance and metrical brilliance. Callimachus stood as the champion of the short poem, witty, erudite, highly polished. The bombast of epic was not for him: "thundering is not my business, but Jupiter's."

CALLIOPE 3.3,4.6. One of the Muses.

CALLISTO 2.28. An Arcadian nymph, loved by Jupiter. He turned her into a she-bear to avoid Juno's notice. She was killed by Diana in a hunt, and became the constellation of the Great Bear.

CALVUS 2.25,2.34. G. Licinius Calvus, born 82 B.C., friend of Catullus who refers (in poem 96) to an elegy written by Calvus on the death of his wife Quintilia; wrote erotic elegy and a narrative poem, the *Io*.

CALYPSO 1.15,2.21. A nymph, daughter of Atlas, who lived on the island of Ogygia, where she entertained the shipwrecked Ulysses for seven years; on the instruction of the gods she reluctantly released him.

CAMILLUS 3.9,3.11. Marcus Furius Camillus. As dictator he saved Rome after the Gallic invasion in 387 B.C.

CAMPANIA 3.5. A fertile area on the west coast of Italy extending from Latium to the Surrentine promontory and including the Bay of Naples. Capua was its chief city.

CANNAE 3.3. A village in Apulia in southern Italy, the site of a battle in 216 B.C. in which Rome suffered a disastrous defeat at the hands of Hannibal.

CANOPUS 3.11. A city in Egypt with a reputation for loose living.

CAPANEUS 2.34. One of the Seven against Thebes; struck with lightning by Jupiter as he attempted to scale the walls of Thebes.

CAPHAREUS 3.7. A rocky promonotory on the coast of Euboea, where the Greek fleet was wrecked on its return from Troy.

CAPITOL 4.4. One of the hills of Rome (otherwise *Mons Tarpeius);* site of Jupiter's most important temple.

CAPRICORN 4.1.ii. One of the signs of the zodiac.

CASSIOPE 1.17. Mother of Andromeda (q.v.); changed into a constellation.

CASTALIAN SPRING 3.3. A spring on Mount Parnassus sacred to Apollo and the Muses.

CASTOR 2.7,2.26a. Son of Tyndareus and Leda, brother of Helen and Pollux; famous as a horseman; deified with his twin brother with whom he served as a guide to sailors.

CATULLUS 2.25,2.34. Gaius Valerius Catullus (84–54 B.C.) wrote lyric, erotic, and epigrammatic poetry; he is famous above all for his love poems addressed to Lesbia.

CAYSTROS 3.22. (mod. Kara-su) A river in Lydia. Ephesus stands at its mouth.

CENTAURS 1.1,2.2,2.6. Somewhat lecherous mythological monsters, half man half horse, who lived in the mountains of Thessaly.

CERAUNIA 1.8.i,2.16. A ridge of mountains in Epirus in the north of Greece.

CERBERUS 3.5,4.5,4.7,4.11. The three-headed dog that guards the entrance to Hades.

CHARON 2.27. Ferryman of the dead across the River Styx into Hades.

CHARYBDIS 3.12. A vast and deadly whirlpool encountered by Ulysses in his wanderings, on the other side of the narrow strait from Scylla.

CIMBRIAN 2.1. The Cimbri were a Germanic tribe destroyed by Marius (q.v.) at the battle of Vercellae in 101 B.C.

CIRCE 2.1,3.12. A famous witch (related to Medea) who turned Ulysses' men into wild beasts.

CITHAERON 3.2,3.15. A mountain in Boeotia sacred to Bacchus and the Muses.

CLAUDIA 4.11. Claudia Quinta. When Cybele (q.v.) was brought to Rome in 205 B.C., the ship which carried her image went aground in the Tiber. Claudia pulled it free single handed and thus cleared herself of suspicion of unchastity.

CLAUDIUS 3.18,4.10. M. Claudius Marcellus. He killed the Gaul Virdomarus in single combat in 222 B.C. thus winning the *Spolia Opima*. In 212 B.C. he conquered Syracuse.

CLITUMNUS 1.20,2.19,3.22. (mod. Clitunno) A river in Umbria.

CLYTEMNESTRA 3.19,4.7. Daughter of Tyndareus, sister of Helen and the Dioscuri, wife of Agamemnon. While Agamemnon was at Troy she became the mistress of Aegisthus; she murdered Agamemnon on his return in revenge for the sacrifice of Iphigenia, and was in turn murdered by her son Orestes.

COCLES 3.11. Horatius Cocles. When the Etruscans were trying to enter Rome, he stood on a wooden bridge over the Tiber and fought them off while the bridge was cut down behind him. The traditions vary as to whether he survived this exploit.

COLCHIS 1.1,1.20,3.22. A region on the eastern shore of the Black Sea, home of Medea and the Golden Fleece.

COLLINE 4.5. Refers to an area of Rome near the Quirinal and Viminal hills. Near the Colline Gate was an area where Vestal Virgins convicted of unchastity were buried alive. It was thus a good place for picking magic herbs.

CONON 4.1.ii. Of Samos, a noted mathematician and astronomer of the 3rd century B.C.

CORA 4.10. An ancient town in Latium.

CORINNA 2.3. A Greek poetess from Boeotia, contemporary with Pindar (early 5th century B.C.).

CORINTH 3.5. A city on the isthmus between the Peloponnese and the rest of Greece; it became an important commercial centre noted for its wealth and its courtesans. It was sacked by Rome in 146 B.C.

CORNELIA 4.11. Daughter of Cornelius Scipio and Scribonia (who later became the wife of Augustus); married to L. Aemilius Paullus Lepidus; died in 16 B.C.

CORVINUS 3.11. Valerius Corvinus. A 4th century Roman, many times consul and twice dictator, with a remarkable list of exploits to his name. One of these was his single combat with a gigantic Gaul. Corvinus won with the help of a raven *(corvus)* who flapped his wings in his opponent's eyes. Hence the name.

CORYDON 2.34. A shepherd in Vergil's *Eclogue II,* lover of Alexis.

COS 4.5. An island in the eastern Aegean famous for its fabrics.

COSSUS 4.10. Aulus Cornelius Cossus. As consul in 428 B.C. he killed Lars Tolumnius of Veii in single combat and thus won the *Spolia Opima.*

CRASSI 2.10,3.4,3.5,4.6. (1) M. Licinius Crassus, trimvii with Pompey and Caesar, defeated and killed by the Parthians at Carrhae in 52 B.C. (2) P. Licinius Crassus, son of the above, also killed at Carrhae.

CREUSA 2.16,2.21. Daughter of Creon, king of Corinth. When Jason married her and abandoned Medea, Medea responded by killing her with a poisoned dress.

CROESUS 2.26b,3.5,3.18. Fabulously wealthy king of Lydia who reigned 560–546 B.C. His kingdom was overrun by Cyrus of Persia.

CUMAE 1.11. An ancient town on the coast of Campania, on the north shore of the Bay of Naples; home of the Sibyl.

CUPID 1.6,1.7,1.9,3.10,3.23. The god of love and the son of Venus. He is represented as a winged boy with a bow and arrows.

CURES 4.4. A town in Italy close to Rome; the ancient capital of the Sabines.

CURIA 4.1. The Senate House at Rome.

CURII 3.3. Three brothers from Alba who fell in a combat with the three Horatii.

CURTIUS 3.11 M. Curtius. He leapt armed and on horseback into a chasm which opened in the Forum, in response to an oracle that said this would ensure that Rome would never be destroyed. The area in the Forum where this was supposed to have occurred was called the Lacus Curtius.

CYBELE 3.17,3.22,4.11. A fertility goddess of Anatolia, worshipped together with her male consort Attis with ecstatic rites which included the clashing of cymbals. As the Great Mother she was introduced into Rome in 205 B.C.

CYCLOPES 2.33.ii,3.2,3.12. A race of one-eyed giants. Ulysses in his wanderings was imprisoned in the cave of one of them (Polyphemus); he got out by making the Cyclops drunk and putting his single eye out with a heated stake. In another story Polyphemus loved a sea nymph, Galatea; he wooed her—successfully according to Propertius' version—by means of his singing.

CYMOTHOE 2.26a. One of the daughters of Nereus, a sea god.

CYRENE 4.6. A Greek town in northern Africa; birthplace of Callimachus.

CYZICUS 3.22. A town in Mysia situated on an island in the Propontis, joined to the mainland by a causeway.

DANAAN 3.9,3.11,4.1.ii. Used as a synonym for Greek.

DANAE 2.20,2.32. Shut up in a tower by her father Acrisius, she was visited there by Jupiter in the form of a shower of gold. The result was Perseus.

DANAUS 2.31. Father of fifty daughters. See Danaids. He emigrated from Egypt and founded Argos. There was a famous Portico of Danaus in the Temple of Palatine Apollo dedicated by Augustus in 28 B.C.

DANAIDS 2.1,4.11. The fifty daughters of Danaus who were forced against their will to marry the fifty sons of Aegyptus. With the one exception of Hypermestre, they all murdered their husbands on the wedding night. For their crime they were condemned to spend eternity filling a leaky urn with water.

DAPHNIS 2.34. A shepherd named in Vergil's *Eclogue* VII.

DARDAN 4.1.i. (i.e., Trojan.) Dardanus was an early king of Troy.

DECIUS 3.11,4.1.i. Publius Decius Mus, consul in 340 B.C. He dedicated his life to his country and rode to his death against the Samnites, thus ensuring a Roman victory. His son of the same name is reputed to have sacrificed his life in the same way in 295 B.C.

DEIDAMIA 2.9a. Daughter of Lycomedes, king of Scyros; and mother of Neoptolemus by Achilles.

DEIPHOBUS 3.1. A minor hero of Troy; son of Priam.

DELOS 2.31,4.6. A small island in the Aegean, sacred to Apollo. According to legend it had been a floating island but became permanently anchored after Apollo's birth there.

DELPHI 3.13. An important religious sanctuary on the southern slopes of Parnassus, above the Gulf of Corinth; the site of the most important oracle of Apollo. *See also* Pythian, Brennus.

DEMOPHOON 2.24. Son of Theseus. On a visit to Thrace he met Phyllis who fell in love with him. He promised to return, but when he did not, she hanged herself.

DEMOSTHENES 3.21. Famous orator of Athens (384–322 B.C.). His father owned a sword factory.

DEUCALION 2.32. He and his wife Pyrrha were the only mortals to survive the Great Flood.

DIANA 2.19,2.28,4.8. An Italian goddess, identified with the Greek Artemis. She was goddess of the woods and of fertility, particularly that of women. She had an important cult in a grove at Aricia and a temple on the Aventine.

DINDYMUS 3.22. A mountain in Mysia sacred to Cybele.

DIRCE 3.15. Wife of Lycus, king of Thebes. For her persecution of Antiope (q.v.) she was tied to a bull by Amphion and Zethus and dragged to her death.

DIS 3.22. A name for the god of the underworld.

DODONA 1.9,2.21. An ancient oracle of Jupiter in Epirus.

DON 2.30a. (Lat. Tanais) A river of Russia flowing into the Sea of Azov.

DORIS 1.17. Daughter of Oceanus, wife of Nereus, and mother of the fifty Nereids.

DOROZANTIAN 4.5. Nothing is known about the Dorozantians; it is perhaps an invented name for an exotic Eastern people.

ELECTRA 2.14a. Daughter of Agamemnon and Clytemnestra. The version that Propertius follows in 2.14a is that of Sophocles' play, *Electra;* after the murder of her father she awaits the return of her brother Orestes in order to take revenge on her mother and Aegisthus. She is falsely informed that her brother is dead, but, while clasping the urn she believes to contain his ashes, she recognizes the living Orestes standing before her.

ELIS 1.8.ii,3.2. An area in the northwest Peloponnese, home of Hippodamia, wife of Pelops. The area included Olympia, where there was an important temple of Jupiter containing a gold and ivory statue by Phidias.

ELYSIUM 4.7. Originally identical with the Isles of the Blessed, situated at the ends of the earth. Later it was a department of the underworld, where the souls of the good were sent after death.

ENDYMION 2.15. A beautiful youth condemned to sleep forever by Jupiter, because of his love for Juno. Diana (the moon) seduced him as he lay asleep on a mountainside.

ENNIUS 3.3,4.1.i. Quintus Ennius (236–169 B.C.) from Calabria in southern Italy; known as "the father of Roman poetry." He wrote poetry of many kinds, but was best known for his national epic, *The Annales*.

EPICURUS 3.21. Famous Greek philosopher (342–270 B.C.), founder of Epicureanism. His school was centred in the garden of his house in Athens. The aims of his philosophy were to free men from fear and anxiety, and to enable them to lead a life of happiness and ease.

ERICHTHON 2.6. Erichthonius was a legendary king of Athens.

ERIPHYLE 2.16. *See* Amphiaraus and Alcmaeon.

ESQUILINE 3.23,4.8. One of the hills of Rome, a fashionable residential area.

ETRURIA 4.2. (mod. Tuscany) An area of Italy north of Latium. From around 650 B.C. the Etruscans were dominant in Latium (the Tarquin dynasty of Rome was of Etruscan origin). During the 5th century there was a bitter struggle for power between Rome and the Etruscans, which continued until the fall of Veii in 396 B.C.

EUBOEA 2.26c,4.1.ii. An island in the Aegean Sea separated from the mainland (Boeotia) by a narrow strait, Euripus.

EUMENIDES 4.11. A Greek name for the Furies, the spirits of punishment and revenge.

EUPHRATES 2.10,3.4,3.11,4.6. (mod. Frat) A river of Syria which joins with the Tigris and empties into the Persian Gulf.

EUROPA 2.28. Sister of Cadmus; mother of Sarpedon and Minos by Jupiter, who took the form of a bull and carried her off to Crete.

EUROTAS 3.14. A river in the Peloponnese, on which Sparta stands.

EURUS 2.26c. The east wind.

EURYTION 2.33.ii. The Centaur who attempted to rape the bride at the wedding of Pirithous and Hippodamia, and thus started the famous fight between the Centaurs and the Lapiths.

EVADNE 1.15,3.13. Wife of Capaneus, one of the Seven against Thebes. She burned herself on his funeral pyre.

EVANDER 4.1. An exile from Arcadia who came to Italy and founded the town of Pallanteum, later the Palatine Hill.

FABIUS 3.3. Quintus Fabius Maximus, nicknamed Cunctator "the delayer." Appointed dictator during the war against Hannibal, he was said to have saved Rome by his delaying tactics.

FALERNIAN 2.33.ii,4.6. A famous wine from Campania.

FERETRIUS 4.10. A surname of Jupiter, probably derived from the verb *ferire* (strike) and meaning "he who strikes" (though Propertius suggests an alternative etymology from *ferre,* meaning "carry" or "win"). When a Roman general killed the enemy commander he dedicated the spoils (known as the *Spoila Opima)* in the Temple of Jupiter Feretrius.

FIDENAE 4.1. (mod. Castel Giubileo) An ancient town of Latium 5 miles from Rome.

GABII 4.1. (mod. Castiglione) An ancient town of Latium 12 miles from Rome.

GALAESUS 2.34. (mod. Galeso) A river in Calabria, southern Italy.

GALATEA 3.2. A sea nymph wooed by the Cyclops Polyphemus.

GALLUS 2.34. A distinguished poet and statesman, contemporary of Vergil, subject of Vergil's *Eclogue X.* He was considered to be the first Latin writer of erotic elegies. He became Prefect of Egypt under Augustus, was recalled and banished, and committed suicide in 26 B.C.

GERYON 3.22. A three-bodied monster, king of Erytheia, a mythical island in the west. One of the Labours of Hercules was to kill Geryon and drive off his cattle.

GETA 4.5. A typical name for a slave in Roman Comedy.

GETAE 4.3. A Thracian tribe on the lower Danube.

GLAUCUS 2.26a. A fisherman of Euboea who became a sea god.

GORGON 2.2,2.25,3.3,4.9. A monster with snakes for hair. Anybody who looked at her eyes was turned to stone. Perseus killed her with the assistance of Athene, who used her head to decorate her shield. The winged horse Pegasus sprang from her blood at her death.

GROVE (Lake of the) 3.22. (mod. Lago Di Nemi) A lake in Latium near the Alban Lake, taking its name from the Grove of Diana at Aricia.

HAEMON (1) 1.15. Son of Pelasgus; father of Thessalus. Haemonian is used as a synonym for Thessalian. (2) 2.8. Son of Creon of Thebes; betrothed to Antigone (q.v.). He committed suicide over her body.

HANNIBAL 3.3,3.11. Leader of the Carthaginians in the Second Punic War. He crossed the Alps and invaded Italy in 218 B.C. and there inflicted some major defeats on the Romans (*see* Cannae). He was eventually defeated in 204 B.C.

HEBE 1.13. The goddess of youth, who became Hercules' wife after his deification.

HECTOR 2.8,2.22a,3.1,3.8,4.6. Son of Priam; husband of Andromache. The greatest Trojan hero in the Trojan War, he was killed in single combat by Achilles, who dragged his body behind his chariot around the walls of Troy.

HELEN 2.1,2.3,2.15,3.8a,3.14. Daughter of Leda and Jupiter, and wife of Menelaus; she was reputed to be the most beautiful woman in the world. Her abduction by Paris led to the Trojan War.

HELENUS 3.1. A minor hero of Troy; son of Priam.

HELICON 2.10,3.3,3.5. A mountain of Boeotia, where the Muses were supposed to dwell. Just below its summit is the spring Hippocrene (q.v.). Ascra, the birthplace of Hesiod, lies on its slopes.

HELLE 2.26a,3.22. Fled with her brother Phrixus on the back of a ram with a golden fleece to escape her stepmother, Ino. Phrixus reached Colchis safely (where the fleece remained guarded by a dragon); Helle fell from the ram into the strait which was named after her—the Hellespont.

HERCULES 1.11,1.13,2.23,3.18,3.22,4.7,4.9,4.10. Son of Jupiter and Alcmene; a hero of immense strength who had to perform twelve Labours (see Geryon, Hesperides, Hydra). Among many other exploits he wrestled with and killed the giant Antaeus, carried the sky on his shoulders (see Atlas), and went on the expedition of the Argonauts (see Hylas).

HERMIONE 1.4. Daughter of Menelaus and Helen; she became the wife of Orestes.

HESIOD 2.10,2.13a. Early Greek poet (c. 800 B.C.) from Ascra in Boeotia, he was author of the *Theogony* and the *Works and Days*. These are didactic epics, one concerned with genealogies of the gods and the creation of the world, the other with agriculture.

HESPERIDES 3.22. Daughters of Hesperus (the evening). They lived on an island in the far west where, with the help of a dragon, they watched over a tree with golden apples. It was one of the Labours of Hercules to pluck these apples.

HIPPOCRENE 3.1. A spring on Mount Helicon, said to have been created when the winged horse Pegasus struck the rock with his hoof.

HIPPODAMIA 1.2. Daughter of Oenomaus. Her father made it a condition of her hand in marriage that he would pursue the would-be husband in his chariot, and if he caught him put him to death. Pelops avoided the fate of his thirteen predecessors by bribing the charioteer Myrtilus to remove his master's lynchpins.

HIPPOLYTE 4.3. An Amazon captured by Theseus, by whom she became the mother of Hippolytus.

HIPPOLYTUS 2.1,4.5. Son of Theseus and the Amazon Hippolyte. Huntsman and worshipper of Artemis, he was noted for sexual abstinence. His stepmother Phaedra fell in love with him; he rejected her in horror, whereupon she committed suicide leaving a note accusing Hippolytus of raping her. Theseus cursed Hippolytus, and Neptune in answer to Theseus sent a monster from the sea. Hippolytus' horses took fright, threw him from his chariot and dragged him to his death.

HORATII 3.3. Three legendary brothers who fought as champions of Rome against three brothers from Alba, the Curiatii (or Curii).

HUNDRED 4.1. The Senate of 100 appointed by Romulus.

HYDRA 2.24. A seven-headed water serpent killed by Hercules. As soon as one of its heads was cut off two grew up in its place.

HYLAS 1.20. Loved by Hercules, whom he accompanied on the voyage of the Argonauts.

HYPANIS 1.12. (mod. Boug) A river that flows into the Black Sea near the Dneiper.

HYPERMESTRE (or HYPERMNESTRA) 4.7. The only one of the daughters of Danaus who did not kill her husband on their wedding night. *See* Danaids.

HYPSIPYLE 1.15, Queen of Lemnos; loved and deserted by Jason.

ICARUS (or ICARIUS) 2.33.ii. An Athenian who was given the vine by Dionysus as a reward for entertaining him. He made wine from it and offered it to some Attic peasants; they concluded they were being poisoned and murdered him. He became the constellation Bootes.

IDA 2.2,2.13b,2.32,3.1,3.17. A mountain in Phrygia near Troy.

IDALIAN 4.6. From Idalium, a city in Cyprus sacred to Venus. Caesar's star is called Idalian in 4.6 because he was supposed to be descended from Venus.

IDES 4.5. In the Roman calendar the thirteenth or fifteenth day of the month.

ILION 3.1. Another name for Troy.

INO 2.28. Daughter of Cadmus; wife of Athamas (*see* Helle). She nursed Dionysus, was driven mad by Juno, leapt into the sea, and became the sea goddess Leucothoe (or Leucothea).

IO 1.3,2.28,2.30b,2.33.i. Daughter of Inachus, loved by Jupiter. She was changed into a heifer, either by Jupiter for concealment, or by Juno for punishment. Juno set Argus (q.v.) over her to watch her and, when he was killed, had her pursued by a gadfly. After extensive wanderings she was restored to human shape by Jupiter in Egypt. She is sometimes identified with Isis (q.v.).

IONIAN SEA 2.26a,3.11,3.21,4.6. The sea that lies between the west coast of Greece and the southern tip of Italy, south of the Adriatic Sea.

IOPE 2.28. There are two heroines of this name: (1) daughter of Iphiclus, wife of Theseus; (2) (also called Cassiope) wife of the Ethiopian king Cepheus.

IPHIGENIA 3.7. Daughter of Agamemnon, sacrificed by him at Aulis to secure fair winds for the expedition against Troy.

ISCHOMACHE 2.2. Apparently the name of a Lapith woman, not found elsewhere.

ISIS 4.5. An Egyptian goddess whose cult was popular at Rome; her worship involved periods of sexual abstinence. She is sometimes identified with Io (q.v.).

ISMARUS 2.33.ii,3.12. A town of Thrace sacked by Ulysses. Maron, priest of Apollo in Ismarus, gave Ulysses a present of unusually strong wine for protecting him and his family. It was this that Ulysses used to get Polyphemus drunk.

ITHACA 3.5. An island in the Ionian Sea, the home of Ulysses. The Ithacan beggar referred to in 3.5 is Irus, a beggar at Ulysses' palace.

ITYS 3.10. Killed by his mother, Philomela, to get vengeance on her husband, Tereus, for raping Procne, her sister. Philomela was turned into a nightingale.

IULUS 4.1.i. The son of Aeneas.

IXION 1.9,4.11. Condemned to spend eternity fixed to a revolving wheel in Tartarus, for the crime of murdering one of his own kin and/or attempting the rape of Juno.

JASON 2.34. Leader of the Argonauts. He returned from Colchis with the Golden Fleece and Medea, the daughter of the king of Colchis. Later he abandoned her to marry Creusa; Medea in her jealous anger killed Creusa and her own children by Jason.

JOCASTA 2.9b. Queen of Thebes, mother and wife of Oedipus. In the commonest version of the story she commits suicide when she discovers who Oedipus is. In Propertius' version she remains alive and witnesses the fatal struggle between her sons, Eteocles and Polynices, for the kingdom of Thebes. Propertius is perhaps also alluding to a version in which she attempted to mediate between her sons and killed herself when she failed.

JUGURTHA 3.5,4.6. King of Numidia in North Africa. He provoked the Romans to war in 112 B.C. and successfully held them at bay until 104 B.C. when he was captured by Marius, led through the streets of Rome, and executed.

JUNO 2.5,2.33.i,3.22,4.1.ii,4.9. Queen of the gods, wife of Jupiter, notoriously jealous of her husband's affairs. She is associated particularly with women and childbirth.

JUTURNA 3.22. The nymph of a spring (the *Fons Iuturnae*) that lies at the foot of the Palatine; Castor and Pollux are supposed to have watered their horses there after the battle of Lake Regillus in 496 B.C.

KALENDS 4.3. The name of the first day of the month in the Roman calendar.

LAIS 2.6. A well-known Corinthian courtesan.

LANUVIUM 4.8. A town in Latium on the Appian Way, about 15 miles southeast of Rome.

LAODAMIA 1.19. Wife of Protesilaus (q.v.).

LAPITHS 2.2. A wild mountain tribe living in Thessaly; they had a famous brawl with the Centaurs on the occasion of the wedding of Pirithous and Hippodamia.

LARES 3.3. Gods of the household, whose images stood in a small shrine by the hearth.

LAVINIA 2.34. Wife of Aeneas; the city of Lavinium on the seacoast of Latium was founded in her honour.

LECHAEUM 3.21. The port of Corinth on the Corinthian Gulf.

LEDA 1.13. Mother of Helen, Castor, and Pollux; the father was Jupiter who visited Leda in the form of a swan.

LEO 4.1.ii. The Lion, one of the signs of the zodiac.

LEPIDUS 4.11. M. Aemilius Lepidus, one of the sons of Cornelia (q.v.); he became consul in A.D. 6.

LESBIA 2.32,2.34. Catullus' mistress, usually identified with Clodia, a woman of noble birth, sister of P. Clodius Pulcher (a political trouble-maker responsible for Cicero's exile), and wife of Q. Metellus Celer (a provincial governor and consul).

LETHE 4.7. A river of the underworld. The traditional belief was that the soul that drank of its waters forgot its past; however, this notion does not seem to be present in Propertius's use of the term in 4.7.

LEUCADIA 2.34. The mistress of the poet Varro (q.v.).

LEUCIPPUS 1.2. Father of Hilaeira and Phoebe, who were abducted by Castor and Pollux.

LEUCOTHOE 2.26a,2.28. (Or Leucothea). *See* Ino.

LIBO 4.11. The cognomen of Cornelia's maternal line; her brother L. Scribonius Libo was consul in 34 B.C.

LIBURNIANS 3.11. An Illyrian people living in modern Croatia, who gave their name to a light, fast warship, which was the characteristic vessel of Augustus' navy.

LIBYA 4.1.ii. The Greek name for Africa. The reference in 4.1.ii is to the oracle of Jupiter Ammon in the Oasis of Siwa.

LINUS 2.13a. A famous singer and musician, sometimes described as the son of Apollo.

LOTUS 3.12. In the course of his wanderings Ulysses came to the land of the Lotus-eaters. Those who had eaten the Lotus forgot their own country and wished to remain in that land forever.

LUCERES 4.1. An Etruscan tribe (followers of Lycmon q.v.) that united with the Ramnes (Latin followers of Romulus q.v.) and the Titii (Sabine followers of Tatius q.v.) to form the first Roman state, after the war with the Sabines.

LUCRINE LAKE 1.11. (mod. Lago Lucrino) A lake on the Campanian coast near Baiae, a fashionable resort area of great scenic beauty.

LUPERCAL 4.1.i. A festival in honour of Pan celebrated annually in February, in which priests with painted faces ran around the city striking any woman they came across with goatskin thongs; this was supposed to promote fertility.

LYCMON 4.1.i,4.2. The Etruscan leader who helped Romulus against the Sabine Tatius (q.v.). The name is formed from the Etruscan word for leader or priest, Lucumo.

LYCORIS 2.34. The name given by the poet Gallus (q.v.) to his mistress. She was an actress in the Mime who went under the stage name of Cytheris; her real name was Volumnia.

LYCURGUS 3.17. King of Thrace. He opposed the worship of Bacchus and drove the god out of his kingdom so that he was forced to take refuge in the sea. As a consequence Lycurgus was driven mad, chopped off his own legs mistaking them for vines, and then killed his son.

LYCUS 3.15. King of Thebes; husband of Dirce (q.v.).

LYDIA 1.6,3.11,3.17,4.7,4.9. A country in the west of Asia Minor noted for its wealth (see Croesus, Pactolus) and its music; one of the centres of the cult of Cybele.

LYSIPPUS 3.9. A fourth century sculptor from Sicyon in Greece, noted for his ability to catch momentary moods and expressions in bronze.

MAEANDER 2.30b,2.34. A river of Asia Minor noted for its winding "meandering" course.

MAECENAS 2.1,3.9. The patron of Propertius, Vergil, and Horace; a close friend and adviser of Augustus. In spite of his wealth, his nobility (he was descended from Etruscan aristocracy), and his political power, he never held public office, but remained an *eques* (knight).

MAENADS 3.8a,3.22,4.4. Female followers of Bacchus (also called Bacchae and Bacchants); they roamed through the mountains, worshipping him with dance and song, wearing ivy and animal skins and carrying the thyrsus. At the climax of their ecstatic rites they tore wild animals to pieces with their bare hands and ate them raw.

MALEA 3.19. A rocky cape at the southernmost point of the Peloponnese particularly dangerous for shipping.

MAMURIUS 4.2. Mamurius Veturius. A legendary craftsman from the time of Numa (q.v.).

MARCIAN 3.2,3.22. The reference is to a famous aqueduct, the Aqua Marcia, built by Q. Marcius Rex in the 2nd century B.C.

MARIUS 2.1,3.2,3.5,3.11. Gaius Marius (157–86 B.C.); conqueror of Jugurtha (q.v.). When the German tribes, the Teutones and Cimbri, made a dangerous incursion into northern Italy, he defeated them at the battles of Aquae Sextiae (102 B.C.) and Vercellae (101 B.C.).

MARON 2.32. The reference is presumably to a gargoyle representing Maron, known from the *Odyssey* as a priest of Apollo and elsewhere as a son of Bacchus.

MARPESSA 1.2. Daughter of Euenus. Idas, son of Aphareus, and Apollo fought over her. Jupiter arbitrated and gave Marpessa the choice. She chose Idas.

MARS 2.32,3.4,4.1.i,4.1.ii. An important Italian deity of great antiquity, originally perhaps a fertility god, but later identified with Greek Ares as the god of war. One of his rites was the October Horse (q.v.).

MAUSOLUS 3.2. 4th century ruler of Caria, a region of Asia Minor. His massive tomb (Mausoleum) was regarded as one of the seven wonders of the world.

MEDEA 2.1,2.21,2.24,2.34,3.11,3.19,4.4,4.5. Daughter of Aeetes, king of Colchis. She fell in love with Jason and helped him to win the Golden Fleece. When Jason married Creusa (q.v.) she killed Creusa and her own children by Jason. She was noted for her powers of witchcraft.

MELAMPUS 2.3. A prophet who attempted to steal the cattle of Iphiclus. These were demanded by Neleus, king of Pylos, as the price of the hand of his daughter Pero. In the usual version, Melampus undertakes the theft for his brother Bias. In Propertius 2.3 he himself appears to be the suitor. Melampus was caught and imprisoned, but was later released and permitted to take the cattle.

MEMNON 2.18a. Son of Aurora, the dawn; king of Ethiopia. He fought on the Trojan side in the Trojan War, and was killed by Achilles.

MEMPHIS 3.11. A city of Egypt and residence of the Egyptian kings (mod. Metrahenny, 14 miles south of Cairo).

MENANDER 2.6,3.21,4.5. The most famous writer of Attic New Comedy (c. 342–291 B.C.). One of his plays was about Thais, an Athenian courtesan.

MENELAUS 2.3,2.15,2.34. King of Sparta, brother of Agamemnon, and husband of Helen.

MENTOR 1.14,3.9. A well-known silversmith of the early 4th century B.C.

MERCURY 2.30a. The messenger god, equivalent to the Greek Hermes. Part of his equipment was a pair of winged sandals.

MEROE 4.6. A city of Ethiopia. The Ethiopians had invaded Egypt in 22 B.C. and been repulsed.

METHYMNA 4.8. A city on the island of Lesbos in the Aegean. It was noted for its wine.

MEVANIA 4.1.ii. (mod. Bevagna) A town in Umbria.

MILANION 1.1. Successful suitor of Atalanta; according to most versions, he defeated her in a foot race by throwing in her path the three golden apples of Venus. In Propertius' version he wins her love by going hunting with her.

MINERVA 1.2,3.20a,4.1.ii. A Roman goddess identified with Athene, goddess of wisdom, poetry, and handicrafts.

MIMNERMUS 1.9. A Greek poet from Colophon in Asia Minor, fl. 630 B.C. He was one of the earliest writers of erotic poetry in the elegiac metre.

MINOS 2.32,3.19,4.11. Son of Jupiter and Europa; king of Crete. He made war against Megara, whose King Nisus was betrayed to him by his daughter Scylla (q.v.); and against Athens to repay the murder of his son Androgeon (q.v.). He demanded a yearly tribute of youths and maidens from Athens whom he fed to the Minotaur, a monster half man half bull, kept in the Labyrinth at Knossos (*see* Pasiphae, Theseus, Ariadne). After his death Minos became one of the judges in the underworld.

MISENUM 1.11. Northern headland of the Bay of Naples.

MISENUS 3.18. One of the followers of Aeneas; a trumpeter, drowned off Cape Misenum.

MOLOSSIAN 4.8. A famous breed of dogs, coming from Epirus in northern Greece.

MUTINA 2.1. (mod. Modena) A town of Cisalpine Gaul blockaded by Antony in 43 B.C. The blockade was lifted when Antony was defeated by Octavian.

MYRRHA 3.19. The daughter of Cinyras, king of Cyprus. She fell in love with her father and consummated her passion by a trick. He discovered the trick, and, as she fled from his anger, she was turned into a myrrh tree.

MYRON 2.31. A 5th century Greek sculptor. He was particularly noted for his representation of animals.

MYS 3.9. A famous Greek silversmith.

MYSIA 1.20. A region in the northeast of Asia Minor.

NAUPLIUS 4.1.ii. King of Euboea. To avenge the death of his son he lured the Greek fleet onto the rocks at Caphareus on its way back from Troy.

NAXOS 3.17. An island in the Aegean Sea; noted for its wine and its worship of Bacchus.

NEPTUNE 1.13,2.16,2.26a,2.26c,3.7. Italian god of water who became identified with the Greek sea god, Poseidon.

NEREUS 3.7. An old sea god, father of the Nereids.

NESAEE 2.26a. One of the Nereids, sea nymphs, daughters of Nereus.

NESTOR 2.13b,2.25. Son of Neleus; lived to a great age. He was over 60 when he took part in the Trojan War. His son Antilochus was killed defending him against Memnon.

NIOBE 2.20,2.31,3.10. Daughter of Tantalus; wife of Amphion. She had six sons and six daughters and boasted she was as good as Latona who had only one of each (Apollo and Artemis). As punishment her children were killed by the children of Latona, and she was turned into a rock on Mount Sipylus in Lydia.

NIREUS 3.18. A Greek who fought at Troy; very handsome, but no fighter.

NOMENTUM 4.10. (mod. Mentana) A Sabine town about 15 miles north east of Rome.

NUMA 4.2. Numa Pompilius, the second king of Rome (traditionally 715–673 B.C.). He was noted for his piety and accredited with many religious reforms.

NUMANTIA 4.11. (mod. Garray) A city of Spain. It was captured and destroyed by Scipio Africanus the Younger in 133 B.C., for which he received the title Numantinus. This Scipio was the son of Aemilius Paullus and was adopted by Scipio Africanus the Older. Cornelia (q.v.), whose death is lamented in 4.11, was the daughter of a Scipio and the wife of an Aemilius Paullus.

OCNUS 4.3. A hard-working man who allowed his wife to waste all his earnings, and was condemned for this to spend eternity making rope out of straw, while a donkey stood by him eternally consuming the product of his labour.

OCTOBER HORSE 4.1.i. A festival of Mars that took place on the 15th of October; after a chariot race in the Campus Martius, one of the winning horses was sacrificed, his tail was cut off, and the blood that dripped from it was used for a purificatory ritual.

OEAGRUS 2.30b. King of Thrace, father of Orpheus. The mother was one of the Muses; history does not relate which.

OENONE 2.32. A nymph on Mount Ida who was loved by Paris, then deserted by him for Helen.

OETA 1.13,3.1. A mountain range between Thessaly and Aetolia, site of Hercules' funeral pyre.

OLBIA 2.7. (mod. Kudak) A town on the Dnieper.

OLYMPUS 2.1. A mountain of northern Greece, the highest peak in Greece. The giants Otus and Ephialtes, in their assault on the gods, piled Mount Ossa on Olympus and Mount Pelion on Ossa in order to reach heaven. Normally Mount Olympus itself is regarded as the abode of the gods.

OMPHALE 3.11. A Lydian queen. At one stage in his career Hercules served as her slave and fell in love with her; according to some versions, she set him to perform women's tasks and dressed him in women's clothing. *See* 4.9.

ORION 2.16,2.26c. A hunter of gigantic stature who became a constellation; its rising and setting were associated with stormy weather.

ORITHYIA 2.26c,3.7. Daughter of Erechtheus, king of Athens, abducted by Boreas, the north wind, by whom she became the mother of Zetes and Calais.

ORPHEUS 2.13a,3.2. Son of a Muse and Oeagrus (or sometimes Apollo); famous as a singer and lyre player who could calm wild beasts and make the trees and stones follow him.

ORTYGIA 3.22. A name for Ephesus, famous for its Temple of Diana which was regarded as one of the seven wonders of the world.

OSCAN 4.2. The Oscans were the inhabitants of Campania, who spoke an Italic dialect, distinct from Latin, which survived in some areas into Imperial times.

OSSA 2.1. A mountain in Thessaly. *See* Olympus.

OX-MEADOWS 4.9. The reference is to the Forum Boarium, an area of Rome between Velabrum (q.v.) and the Tiber. The name is supposed to come from the Latin *bos* (an ox or cow), because Hercules fed his cattle there.

PACTOLUS 1.6,1.14,3.18. A river in Lydia whose sands were reputed to be rich in gold.

PAESTUM 4.5. A town on the coast of Lucania in southern Italy, famous for its rose gardens.

PAGASAE 1.20. A coastal town of Thessaly, where the Argo was built.

PALATINE 4.1,4.6,4.9. One of the hills of Rome; according to tradition the earliest settlement was made here (*see* Evander). It was the site of the Palace of the Emperor and of a Temple and Portico of Apollo dedicated by Augustus in 28 B.C. (See 2.31).

PALLAS 2.2,3.9,4.4,4.9. A title of Athene, identified with Minerva.

PAN 1.18,3.3,3.13,3.17. An Arcadian god, son of Mercury, with the legs, ears, and horns of a goat; a fertility spirit, god of nature in the wild, and of hunting; a lover of mountains and lonely places (the inducer of panic); amorously inclined (among others, he loved Pitys, the nymph of the pine tree); and musical (his instrument being the pan-pipe).

PANCRATION 3.14. An athletic contest which involved both boxing and wrestling.

PARILIA 4.1,4.4. A country festival held on April 21, traditionally regarded as the date of Rome's foundation. A purificatory ritual which involved, among other things, the lighting of straw bonfires over which the celebrants jumped three times.

PARIS 2.3,2.15,2.32,3.1,3.8a,3.13. Son of Priam. He loved and deserted the nymph Oenone, and was judge in a beauty contest between Juno, Athene, and Venus, awarding victory to the last. Venus gave him Helen as his reward; he abducted her from Sparta and this led to the Trojan War. He was a bowman, not noted for his military exploits, but responsible for the death of Achilles.

PARNASSUS 2.31,3.13. A mountain in Phocis (central Greece), sacred to Apollo and the Muses; Delphi and the Castalian Spring lie on its slopes.

PARRHASIUS 3.9. A famous Greek painter of the late 5th century B.C.

PARTHIA 2.10,2.14,2.27,3.4,3.9,3.12,4.3,4.5,4.6. A powerful empire on the eastern flank of the Roman Empire, extending from the Euphrates to the Indus, with its capital at Ecbatana. The battle of Carrhae in 53 B.C. with the loss of Roman standards and the life of the Triumvir Crassus (q.v.) was a serious blow to Roman pride; but the expedition frequently hinted at by Propertius never took place (at least not till the reign of Trajan). The lost standards were recovered by diplomacy in 20 B.C.

PASIPHAE 2.28,3.19,4.7. Wife of Minos of Crete. She fell in love with a bull and, to persuade him to return her affections, disguised herself as a cow. The product of this union was the Minotaur.

PATROCLUS 2.1,2.8. The squire and close friend of Achilles. Wearing the armour of Achilles he was killed by Hector, whereupon Achilles, grief stricken, returned to the battlefield and took a bloody revenge on Hector and the Trojans.

PAULLUS 4.11. (1) Husband of Cornelia, L. Aemilius Paullus Lepidus, consul suffectus in 34 B.C. and censor in 22 B.C. (2) Son of the above and of Cornelia (consul in A.D. 1, later executed for conspiracy against Augustus).

PEGASUS 2.30a. A winged horse who sprang from the blood of the dying Gorgon; springs gushed forth where he stamped his hoof (see Hippocrene). He was caught and tamed by Bellerophon.

PELEUS 2.9a. Father of Achilles.

PELION 2.1,3.22. A mountain in Thessaly. *See* Olympus.

PELOPS 1.8.ii,3.19,4.6. Son of Tantalus; successful suitor of Hippodamia (q.v.). His action in throwing Myrtilus into the sea resulted in a curse being called down on his house; this worked itself out in the stories of Agamemnon, Clytemnestra, and Orestes.

PELUSIUM 3.9. A city on the eastern mouth of the Nile captured by Octavian in 30 B.C.

PENELOPE 2.9a,3.12,3.13,4.5. Wife of Ulysses; remained faithful to him during his twenty years of absence (at Troy and on the return journey) in spite of a house full of suitors.

PENTHESILEA 3.11. An Amazon queen who fought at Troy. She was killed by Achilles who fell in love with her as she lay dying.

PENTHEUS 3.17,3.22. King of Thebes, who refused to admit the divinity of Bacchus when he returned to his native city. For this he was driven mad, and Agave his mother and the women of Thebes tore him to pieces in a Bacchic frenzy.

PERILLUS 2.25. A famous Athenian craftsman who made a brazen bull for Phalaris tyrant of Agrigentum (570–554 B.C.), to roast his opponents in; the first person to be so disposed of was Perillus.

PERIMEDE 2.4. A representative name for a witch.

PERO 2.3. Daughter of Neleus; loved by Melampus (q.v.).

PERSEPHONE 2.28. Daughter of Demeter; queen of the underworld; wife of Hades. *See* Pluto.

PERSES 4.11. Last king of Macedon, who boasted descent from Achilles. He was defeated and captured by Aemilius Paullus (ancestor of the Cornelia in 4.11 and of her husband) at the battle of Pydna in 168 B.C.

PERSEUS 2.28,2.30a,3.22. Son of Jupiter and Danae. He cut off the Gorgon's head with the help of Athene; rescued Andromeda (q.v.) and married her. Mercury lent him his winged sandals.

PERUGIA 1.22. A town of Etruria, site of a minor but savage incident in the Civil War; in 41 B.C. it harboured L. Antonius, and was captured and plundered by Octavian.

PHAEACIANS 3.2. The people of Scherie, kingdom of Alcinous (q.v.).

PHAEDRA 2.1. Wife of Theseus, stepmother of Hippolytus (q.v.).

PHIDIAS 3.9. Famous 5th century Athenian sculptor. His works included a gold and ivory statue of Zeus (Jupiter) at Olympia.

PHILETAS 2.34,3.1,3.9,4.6. Late 4th century Greek poet from Cos; writer of epigrams, elegies, and epyllia; highly influential both on the Alexandrians and on the Roman elegists. Only fragments of his works survive.

PHILIP 3.11. Philip of Macedon, father of Alexander the Great, was the ancestor of the kings of Macedon who fought against Rome (see Perses), and of the Ptolemies, the royal dynasty of Egypt.

PHILIPPI 2.1. A city in Macedonia; site of the battle in 42 B.C. in which Antony defeated Brutus and Cassius.

PHILOCTETES 2.1. Celebrated archer and companion of Hercules who gave him at his death arrows without which Troy could not be taken. He was bitten by a snake en route to Troy, and abandoned on the island of Lemnos because of the stench of the wound. Ulysses tricked him into coming to Troy where his wound was healed. He killed Paris with his arrows.

PHINEUS 3.5. A king of Thrace who was plagued by the Harpies (monsters who were half bird and half woman) for blinding his children. They prevented him from eating by stealing or defiling his food.

PHLEGRAEAN PLAIN 2.1,3.9,3.11. A plain either in Thessaly or in Italy near Naples; the legendary site of the battle of the gods and giants. The reference in 3.11 is either to the battle of Pharsalus where Pompey was defeated by Caesar in 48 B.C., or to Naples where Pompey almost died of an illness in 50 B.C.

PHOEBUS 2.15,2.32,3.12,3.20b,3.22,4.1. A name for Apollo meaning the Shining One. In 3.12 Phoebus' daughter is Lampetie who looked after the Cattle of the Sun which were killed for food by Ulysses' men.

PHOENIX 2.1. Son of Amyntor. He was persuaded by his mother to sleep with his father's concubine, was discovered, and (in one version of the story) blinded by his father. He was finally cured by the Centaur Chiron. Exiled from his home, he became tutor of Achilles whom he accompanied to Troy.

PHRYGIA 4.6. An area of northwest Asia Minor in which Troy was located; home of the flute.

PHRYNE 2.6. A famous courtesan from Thespiae in the 4th century. She offered to rebuild Thebes at her own expense after it was destroyed by Alexander, with an inscription that read "DESTROYED BY ALEXANDER. RESTORED BY PHRYNE."

PHYLLIS 2.24. Loved by Demophoon son of Theseus; when he deserted her, she killed herself.

PIERIA 2.10. A region of Macedonia, site of one of the most ancient cults of the Muses.

PINDAR 3.17. A famous Greek lyric poet from Boeotia (518-438 B.C.), remarkable for the power and sublimity of his language.

PINDUS 3.5. (mod. Mezzara) A high mountain in Thessaly.

PIRAEUS 3.21. The port of Athens, about four miles from the city, with which it was formerly connected by the Long Walls.

PIRITHOUS 2.1,2.6. A Lapith, son of Jupiter. He was a close friend of Theseus and accompanied him on his descent to the underworld. There was a famous brawl between Centaurs and Lapiths at his marriage with Hippodamia.

PISCES 4.1.ii. The Fishes, one of the signs of the zodiac.

PLATO 3.21. The famous Athenian philosopher (c. 429–347 B.C.); he founded a school called the Academy in a park and gymnasium named after the hero Academus.

PLEIADS (or PLEIADES) 1.8.i,2.16,3.5. A constellation of seven stars associated with rainy and stormy weather.

PLUTO 2.28. Identical with Hades, lord of the underworld and king of the dead. He abducted Persephone as she was picking flowers, forcing her to spend part of the year below ground.

PO 1.12. The largest river in Italy, which flows into the Adriatic near Ravenna.

POLYDAMAS 3.1. A minor Trojan hero in the Trojan War.

POLLUX 3.22. Twin brother of Castor (q.v.); a famous boxer.

POLYMESTOR 3.13. King of Thrace, son-in-law of Priam. When Polydorus, the youngest son of Priam, was sent to stay with him during the Trojan War, he murdered him for his gold.

POMPEY 2.32,3.11,4.8. Gnaeus Pompeius Magnus, 106–48 B.C., famous Roman general and statesman, defeated by Caesar in 48 B.C. at the battle of Pharsalus and murdered as he landed in Egypt. He built a famous Portico in the Campus Martius in 53 B.C.

PORTA CAPENA 4.3. The gate by which the Appian Way enters Rome.

PRAENESTE 2.32. (mod. Palestrina) A town about 20 miles east of Rome famous for its oracle.

PRAXITELES 3.9. A famous 4th century Athenian sculptor, who did much of his work in Pentelic (Attic) marble.

PRIAM 2.3,2.28,4.1.i. Aged king of Troy at the time of the Trojan War.

PROMETHEUS 2.1,3.5. A Titan, who stole fire for mortals and was punished by being chained on the Caucasus with an eagle to eat his liver daily. Prometheus is also said to have molded man from clay.

PROPONTIS 3.22. The Sea of Marmora lying between the Hellespont and the Bosporus.

PROTESILAUS 1.19. A Thessalian, who went to Troy knowing that he was fated to be the first man killed. His newly-wed wife Laodamia grieved so much at his death that the gods allowed her to see him again for three hours. When the time was up, she committed suicide.

PYRRHUS 3.11. King of Epirus (319–272 B.C.). He helped the people of Tarentum against the Romans, and in the course of the war won a number of victories but at great cost (hence "Pyrrhic Victory"). After the drawn battle of Beneventum he returned to Epirus.

PYTHIAN 2.31. A title of Apollo, also of his priestess at Delphi, derived from the Python, former occupant of the oracle, whom Apollo slew.

PYTHON 4.6. The snake that occupied the oracle at Delphi and was killed by Apollo.

QUINTILIA 2.34. Wife (or perhaps mistress) of the poet Calvus (q.v.).

QUIRINUS 4.6,4.10. A god, perhaps of Sabine origin, worshipped from early times on the Quirinal Hill at Rome. Romulus is sometimes identified with him.

RAMNES 4.1. One of the three original Roman tribes. *See* Luceres.

REMUS 2.1,3.9,4.1.i. Brother of Romulus (q.v.), sometimes identified with him.

ROMULUS 2.6,4.1.i,4.4,4.6,4.10. Legendary founder of Rome, with his brother Remus. Exposed as babies, they were suckled by a she-wolf and brought up by a herdsman. Intending to found a city on the site of Rome, they watched for birds to give them the proper omens, Romulus on the Palatine, Remus on the Aventine. Romulus was successful and built a wall; Remus in scorn and pique jumped over it, and Romulus (or a lieutenant of his) killed him. After a reign of 40 years, Romulus was taken up to heaven in a storm and became the god Quirinus (q.v.).

SABINES 2.32,4.2,4.4,4.9. A tribe of unknown origin settled northeast of Rome. The Romans fought a series of wars with them from early times until 449 B.C. when Rome won a major victory. According to legend, Romulus provided women for his newly founded settlement by inviting the Sabines to a festival, then kidnapping their women (the so-called Rape of the Sabines—see Tatius). The Romans appear to have been influenced by the Sabines in a number of their religious practices.

SACRED WAY 2.1,2.23,2.24,3.4. A busy street in Rome with many stores on it; it ran through the centre of the city past the Forum Romanum, its name coming from the sacred buildings that lay on its route (such as the Temple of Vesta and the Palace of Numa). A triumphal procession passed along it before ascending the Capitol.

SATURN 2.32,4.1.ii. An ancient Roman deity who becomes in mythology the father of Jupiter. The period when he was king in heaven was thought of as a golden age. He was also one of the signs of the zodiac.

SCAEAN GATE 3.9. The western gate of Troy, before which the duel between Achilles and Hector took place.

SCAMANDER 3.1. One of the rivers of the plain of Troy, also called Xanthus; according to legend the offspring of Jupiter.

SCIPIO 3.11. A distinguished Roman family of the Gens Cornelia; the main reference in 3.11 is probably to the invasion of Africa in 204 B.C. by Scipio Africanus Major.

SCIRON 3.16,3.22. A legendary thug who terrorized travellers on the Scironian Way between Athens and Megara. He made them wash his feet, and, as they did so, kicked them over the cliff. Theseus threw him into the sea.

SCRIBONIA 4.11. Mother of Cornelia (q.v.); wife of Cornelius Scipio. Later she became the wife of Augustus for a brief period.

SCYLLA (1) 2.26c,3.12. A sea monster with six hands and twelve feet living in a cave opposite Charybdis (q.v.); a ring of dogs grew from her loins. She was encountered by Ulysses on his return from Troy. (2) 3.19. Daughter of Nisus, king of Megara. She fell in love with Minos who was attacking Megara, and betrayed her father by cutting off his purple lock of hair.

In 4.4. Propertius appears to conflate these two stories.

SCYTHIA 1.6,1.8.i,3.16,4.3. An area of southern Russia, between the Carpathians and the Don.

SEMELE 2.28,2.30b. Daughter of Cadmus, king of Thebes; mother of Bacchus by Jupiter. *See* Bacchus.

SEMIRAMIS 3.11. A semi-legendary queen of Assyria (probably identical to Queen Sammuramat, regent of Assyria 810–805 B.C.), famous for having built (or rebuilt) Babylon.

SIBYL 2.2,2.24,4.1.i. A name for an ecstatic prophetess; in particular the reference is to the Sibyl at Cumae, prophetess of Apollo, who was consulted by Aeneas on his arrival in Italy. She was condemned to live for 1,000 years; as she grew older and smaller she hung in a vessel, and, when asked what she wanted, replied "I want to die."

SILENUS 2.32,3.3. The Sileni were spirits of nature, inhabiting the woods and hills, having characteristics of horses and goats, very similar to satyrs. They became associated with Bacchus. Father Silenus is conventionally represented as an ugly, randy, but wise and sensitive old man. (Socrates was compared to him in ancient times).

SIMOIS 2.9a,3.1. One of the rivers of the plain of Troy.

SINIS 3.22. A legendary thug who lived on the Corinthian isthmus. His method of disposing of passers-by was to bend down pine trees and either (a) catapult people into the air, or (b) attach them to two trees so that they were torn apart when the trees were released. He was killed by Theseus by the same treatment.

SIRENS 3.12. Half women half birds with beautiful voices. Sailors, unable to resist their song, landed on their island and were destroyed. Ulysses got past them by stopping up the ears of his men with wax and being himself bound to the mast of his ship.

SISYPHUS 2.17,2.20,4.11. He was tormented in Hades by having to roll a rock up a hill, only to have it roll down again just before reaching the top. It is not clear what his offence was, but he seems to have established a considerable reputation as a crook.

SUBURA 4.6. The "red light" district of Rome, lying between the Viminal and the Esquiline Hills.

SUEBI 3.3. A Germanic tribe. They crossed the Rhine in 29 B.C. and suffered defeat at the hands of the Romans.

STYX 2.9,2.27,3.18. One of the rivers of the underworld. It is normally this river over which Charon ferries the dead.

SYGAMBRI 4.6. A Germanic tribe who defeated the Romans in 16 B.C., but soon after were forced to retreat and give hostages.

SYLVANUS 4.4. A Roman god of the woods.

SYPHAX 3.11. A Numidian king who joined the Carthaginians against Rome at the end of the second Punic War, and was defeated and captured in 203 B.C.

SYRTES 3.19,3.24. Sandbanks off the north African coast notoriously dangerous to shipping.

TANTALUS 2.1,2.17,4.11. Son of Jupiter; father of Pelops. For some offence (in one version, stealing the food of the gods) he was condemned in Hades to be "tantalised": tortured by hunger and thirst, he stood in a stream of water, with fruit hanging from trees over his head; but as he tried to eat or drink the fruit and water disappeared.

TARPEIA 3.11,4.1,4.4,4.8. A Vestal Virgin who betrayed Rome to the Sabines for love of Tatius (q.v.); her story is told in 4.4. She gave her name to the Tarpeian Rock, an overhanging cliff near the Capitol, from which murderers and traitors were thrown.

TARQUIN 3.11. The reference is to Tarquinius Superbus (Tarquin the Proud) the last king of Rome, supposed to have been expelled by Brutus in 510 B.C.

TATIUS 2.32,4.1,4.2,4.4. A Sabine king; after the Rape of the Sabines (see Sabines) he occupied the Capitol; however, the women brought about a reconciliation, and Romulus and Tatius ruled jointly.

TAYGETUS 3.14. A high mountain above Sparta.

TELEGONUS 2.32. Son of Circe and Ulysses; legendary founder of Tusculum, a town about 15 miles southeast of Rome.

TELEPHUS 2.1. King of Mysia, wounded by Achilles; the wound was cured by the application of rust from the spear that had delivered it.

TEUTONES 3.3. A Germanic tribe defeated by Marius at Aquae Sextiae in 102 B.C. *See* Marius.

THAIS 2.6,4.5. A famous Athenian courtesan, subject of a play by Menander.

THAMYRAS 2.22a. A Thracian bard, who challenged the Muses to a competition. The terms of the challenge were that if he won, he could have intercourse with them one after another; if he lost, they could take from him what they wished. He lost, and they took his sight.

THEBES (1) 1.7,2.8,3.2,3.17,3.18. The chief city of Boeotia in central Greece, an important centre in Mycenean times, and the subject of many legends.

(2) 4.5. A city in Egypt, formerly its capital.

THERMODON 4.4. A river in Pontus on the Black Sea; abode of the Amazons (q.v.).

THESEUS 2.1,2.14a,2.24,3.21. King of Athens, slayer of the Minotaur (*see* Minos), lover of Ariadne (q.v.), father of Hippolytus (q.v.) by the Amazon Hippolyte, husband of Phaedra (q.v.), close friend of Pirithous (q.v.).

THESSALY 1.5,1.8.i.1.19,3.11. An area of northern Greece famous for its horses and witches.

THETIS 3.7. The mother of Achilles; a sea goddess.

THYRSIS 2.34. A shepherd named in Vergil's *Eclogue* VII.

TIBER 1.14,2.33.i,3.11,4.1.i,4.2,4.10. The river that runs through Rome.

TIBUR 2.32,3.16. (mod. Tivoli) A town 18 miles north east of Rome, famous as a beauty spot for its hills, woods, and especially the falls on the river Anio.

TIGRIS 3.4. A river flowing from Armenia to the Persian Gulf, east of the River Euphrates.

TIRESIAS 4.9. A legendary prophet of Thebes, blinded when he saw Athene bathing.

TISIPHONE 3.5. One of the Furies, the spirits of punishment and revenge.

TITANS 2.1,3.9. Children of Heaven and Earth, a generation senior to the Olympian gods. There was a violent struggle between the Titans and the following generation, which resulted in the victory of Jupiter.

TITHONUS 2.18a,2.25. Husband of Aurora, the Dawn, granted immortality but not eternal youth.

TITII 4.1.i. One of the three original tribes of Rome. *See* Luceres.

TITYRUS 2.34. A shepherd named in Vergil's *Eclogue* I.

TITYUS 3.5. A giant who was killed by Apollo for trying to rape Leto; he was stretched out in the underworld covering an area of nine *iugera* (a Roman measure somewhat larger than an acre) while a vulture consumed his liver.

TIVOLI 3.22,4.7. *See* Tibur.

TOLUMNIUS 4.10. A king of Veii killed by Cossus (q.v.).

TRITON 2.32,4.6. A sea god or merman often depicted blowing a conch.

TUSCAN 1.21,1.22,3.17. i.e., from Etruria.

TUSCANY ROW 4.2. Vicus Tuscus, a street in Rome running into the Forum.

TWINS 1.17. The Dioscuri, Castor and Pollux (q.v.).

TYNDARIS 2.32. Daughter of Tyndareus; a name for Helen. Tyndareus was the husband of Leda.

TYRE 2.16,4.5. A city on the Phoenician coast, famous for the purple dye extracted from the murex, a shell fish found in its waters.

TYRO 1.13,2.28,3.19. Daughter of Salmoneus, who fell in love with the river Enipeus. She was impregnated by Neptune masquerading as Enipeus, and became the mother of Neleus and Peleus.

ULYSSES 1.15,2.9a,2.14a,2.26c,3.7,3.12. (or Odysseus) King of Ithaca, whose adventures on his return journey from Troy are described in Homer's *Odyssey*.

UMBRIA 1.22,3.22,4.1i,4.1.ii. A district of Italy northeast of Rome; birthplace of Propertius.

VARRO 2.34. P. Terentius Varro Atacinus, 82–c.35 B.C. A poet who wrote love elegies to his mistress Leucadia, also a translation or imitation of Apollonius Rhodius' epic, *The Argonautica*.

VEII 4.10. The most important city of Etruria (q.v.), nine miles north of Rome; for a long time it was Rome's chief opponent, finally taken in 396 B.C.

VELABRUM 4.9. An area in Rome between the Capitol and the Palatine. In early times it was covered by the waters of the Tiber, but later it became one of the busiest parts of the city.

VERGIL 2.34. A famous Roman poet, elder contemporary of Propertius; author of the *Eclogues* (short pastoral poems), the *Georgics* (a didactic poem on agriculture and the farmer's life), and the *Aeneid* (an epic that describes Aeneas' flight from Troy and his arrival in Italy to found the Roman nation).

VERTUMNUS 4.2. An Etruscan god taken over by Rome. His statue stood in the *Vicus Tuscus (see* Tuscany Row); a god of crops and of commercial exchange.

VESTA 2.29.ii,3.4,4.1.i,4.4,4.11. Roman goddess of the hearth. In the state cult her flame was tended by six Vestal Virgins who served for 30 years; the penalty for unchastity was to be buried alive.

VIRDOMARUS 4.10. A Gallic chieftain killed by Claudius Marcellus in 222 B.C. *See* Claudius.

VOLSINII 4.2. (mod. Bolsana) A town in Etruria.

XERXES 2.1. King of Persia from 485–465 B.C. He mounted a massive expedition against Greece, but was defeated at the battles of Salamis and Plataea. In the course of the expedition he cut a canal through the promontory of Athos in Macedonia.

ZETES 1.20. Son of Boreas, the north wind. *See* Calais.

ZETHUS 3.15. Son of Antiope (q.v.); brother of Amphion.